FOR OUR ANGEL,

JOHN GAGGIN

The Gay Man's Guide to Heterosexuality

St. Martin's Griffin

New York

The Gay Man's Guide to Heterosexuality

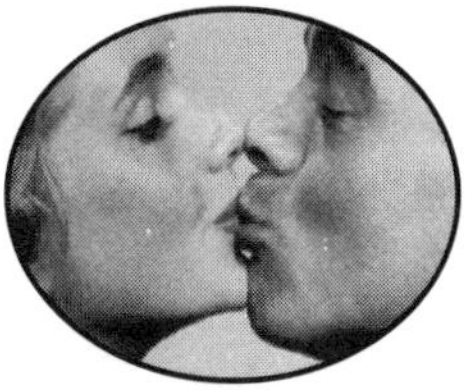

C.E. Crimmins
and Tom O'Leary

For information, address St. Martin's Press, 175 Fifth Avenue, New York, N.Y. 10010.

Design by Songhee Kim

Library of Congress Cataloging-in-Publication Data

Crimmins, C.E.
The gay man's guide to heterosexuality / by C.E. Crimmins and Tom O'Leary.
p. cm.
ISBN 0-312-18102-7
1. Gay men—Humor. 2. Heterosexual men—Humor.
I. O'Leary. Tom, II. Title.
PN6231.H57C75 1998
818'.5407—dc21 97-46093
CIP

First edition: April 1998

10 9 8 7 6 5 4 3 2 1

CONTENTS

ACKNOWLEDGMENTS

Of course, we owe everything to the marvelous staff of the Institute for Heterosexual Studies, which supported us for years in our research. And thanks especially to Biff, the trained chimp who typed the manuscript.

Tom acknowledges C.E. the Dominatrix, and C.E. acknowledges Tom the Needy. (We don't know exactly for what. . . .) We both acknowledge our amazing ability to goof around for hours doing no writing whatsoever.

Many thanks to Rick Morin, Gary and Kevin and The Revere Guest House in Provincetown. Thanks also to Padric Meagher and Michael Guy, Kevin Glaccum and Andi, Park Walkup and Edward J. Perreault, Glenn Esher, Chris Hottle, Rob Michaels, Matthew Stuart, Bob Subb, Phil and Kenneth, George B. and Mitch, Wil Roche, Martin Blair, Tom Tvrdy and Keith, Dr. Edmund Cyvas, and Eric Mortenson for providing the original inspiration with his probing question, "What *do* heterosexuals do in bed?"

In gay, wild, and free Philadelphia, our appreciation goes to Joellen Brown, Kelly Crimmins, Alan Forman, Sarah and Joanne Babaian, St. James Shatzer, Jim Schank, Elizabeth Kelly Crimmins, and Tom Maeder for putting up with one of the authors. Guess who?

We also want to thank that wonderful writer and friend, Barbara Seaman, the book's fairy godmother.

Finally, many thanks to our agent, Frank Weimann, to his amazing accomplice, Cathy McCormac, and to editor Michael Denneny for taking a chance on two adorable, crazy kids with a mighty high concept.

HETEROSEXUALITY IS A FAILURE OF STYLE.

—NOEL COWARD

A MESSAGE FROM THE INSTITUTE FOR HETEROSEXUAL STUDIES

Dear Reader,

You've tried to ignore them. It's never worked.

You think they'll go away. They didn't. They haven't. They won't.

Heterosexuals are not just a passing phase.

THEY'RE HERE TO STAY!

At the Institute for Heterosexual Studies, our mission is to help interpret this strange culture. We want to help you learn more about this odd lifestyle.

We encourage you to use this book to get over your fear—and perhaps loathing—of heterosexuals. Good luck. (And, by the way, if you have any unusual observations or anecdotes to contribute to our growing documentation on this rare sector of society, please contact our publisher.)

The Gay Man's Guide to Heterosexuality

1. Welcome to Heteroland!

Who are heterosexuals? Where do they live?

Do they speak a different language?

Can I interact with them safely?

Heterosexuals: Who Are They?

A heterosexual person is someone who is attracted to the opposite sex. Chances are you already know several. Some of your coworkers, friends, and even your parents could be heterosexually inclined. Your priest may be a heterosexual, although that is highly doubtful.

You may also know heterosexuals by their more familiar names, "straights" or "breeders." Or you may have heard their sexual preference referred to as "the love that *dares* to speak its name"—over, and over, and OVER again.

No one knows what makes a person heterosexual, though we have many theories. Recent studies are making a convincing case for the existence of a heterosexual gene. But environmental factors cannot be totally discounted. (Some experts believe that heterosexual men are overidentified with their dominating fathers!) And, hard as it is to believe, some experts have suggested that heterosexuality is not biologically based, but a free choice.

Where Do You Find Them?

You can bump into them anywhere. Sightings occur daily at shopping malls, amusement parks, fast-food restaurants, car dealerships, sporting events, and even your local supermarket. When you see a heterosexual, remain calm. If you don't make any sudden moves, they'll go about their business as usual and not harm you. But if you call attention to yourself, they are liable to panic and could hurt you. Just as with zoo animals, you should never feed them (unless you work in a restaurant).

Where Do They Live?

While you might see heterosexuals out and about, you are probably less familiar with their home habitats. They have their own special enclaves—you'll be able to spot them better if you use this handy checklist.

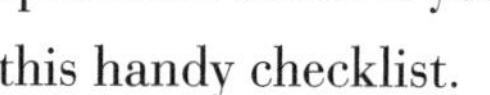

WHAT YOU WILL SEE IN A HETEROSEXUAL NEIGHBORHOOD

- ❑ Tricycles on the lawns
- ❑ Pickup trucks
- ❑ Mary Kay Cosmetics representatives
- ❑ Satellite dishes
- ❑ Chuck E. Cheese, Toys "R" Us, and Ponderosa Steak Houses
- ❑ Pumpkin trash bags

How Do They Amuse Themselves?

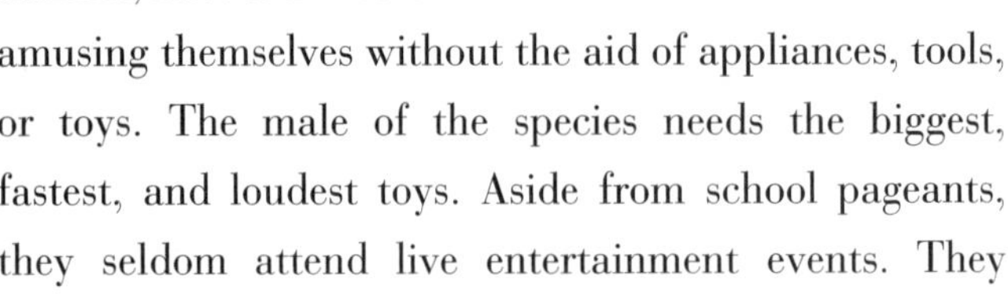

Here at the Institute we have spent years studying the peculiar pleasure patterns of straight people. Heterosexuals, not known for their wit or conversational abilities, have a difficult time amusing themselves without the aid of appliances, tools, or toys. The male of the species needs the biggest, fastest, and loudest toys. Aside from school pageants, they seldom attend live entertainment events. They spend an inordinate amount of time watching television, a mythical medium that reinforces their cultural self-esteem while letting them know what is on sale at the mall.

Heterosexual Myths

Myths abound when it comes to heterosexuals. We could fill a whole book with them, but in the interest of space considerations we will explore just a few major misconceptions.

MYTHS ABOUT HETEROSEXUALS: TRUE OR FALSE?

HETS are environmentally unsafe.
True. A lot of them pollute planet Earth with McDonald's Happy Meal toys and disposable diapers.

HETS are unnatural deviants.
True. Who else would think Howard Stern is funny?

HETS are handy.
False. Although many of them seem to be fixing things, this minor talent far from offsets the major

hetero technical disasters such as Chernobyl, the *Challenger* space shuttle, and the Pinto.

HETS are not to be trusted around children.
True. Child abuse and dysfunctional families are the legacy of rampant heterosexuality. More kids are screwed up by heterosexuals than by any other special-interest group.

HETS are size-obsessed.
True. But only where ego is concerned.

HETS are backbiting.
True. In fact, we would go so far as to caution spending time face-to-face only.

HETS are afraid of hair products.
True.

HETS are boring.
False. After all, they have given us *Doctor Quinn, Medicine Woman*, Jerry Lewis, and Epcot Center.

HETS don't age well.
False. Cosmetic surgery has turned back the clock at

least half an hour for many straight icons, including Cher, George Hamilton, and Jane Fonda.

HETS are afraid of small dogs.
True.

What Language Do They Speak?

Our linguistics experts have spent years studying the peculiar dialect of heterosexuals, or what we call "heterospeak." Heterospeak is loud, direct, devoid of irony, and lacking in lyricism. Some scholars would classify it as a language, but those are the same people who might recommend teaching ebonics in school. Because the language barrier could keep you from understanding the nuances of het culture, we offer a short course in beginning heterospeak.

HETEROSPEAK 101: THE BASICS

Guttural noises are the building blocks of the hetero male vocabulary. These inarticulate expressions of need, anger, and desire might seem the most difficult for a sophisticated gay speaker to master. Yet once you become fluent in the heterosexual male grunt, you will be surprised at how much easier it becomes to communicate with the natives.

PRACTICE THE FOLLOWING PHRASE TRANSLATIONS DAILY:

HOMO: Yes, I would love another cocktail.
HETERO: uhngh

HOMO: You are the love of my life.
HETERO: uhngh

HOMO: Yes, dear, I am famished.
HETERO: uhngh

HOMO: Yes, that shade of green highlights your eyes.
HETERO: uhngh

HETEROSPEAK 102: MORE COMPLICATED PHRASES

In those situations when heterosexual males feel prompted to use words, they do so sparingly. It's almost as if they're speaking in telegrams and being charged a fee for each word. If you are to advance in hetspeak, you must practice the following pared-down phrases:

HOMO: Yes, I agree with your opinion of that film.
HETERO: Yeah.

HOMO: The art museum? Just take the next left and go two blocks and it's that neoclassical building on the right.
HETERO: (pointing) Uhhh . . . that way.

HOMO: I'd rather you tell me something I didn't know.
HETERO: No shit.

HETEROSPEAK 103: THE ADVANCED COURSE

Congratulations! You are now ready for complex sentences that you will be able to use in many situations.

HOMO: You go, girl!
HETERO: Thataway, bud!

HOMO: She is working my very last nerve.
HETERO: He really fuckin' pissed me off.

HOMO: Daniel is multi-exclusively snow queen city.
HETERO: Danny only does white chicks.

HOMO: Such a cruise I got on the IRT this morning.
HETERO: This broad was lookin' right at me.

HOMO: Want to come home and hear my Dusty CDs?
HETERO: Wanna come home and watch my Michael Jordan tapes?

HOMO: What is the 411 on that poodle on your head?
HETERO: Hey man, did you do somethin' to your hair?

HOMO: Hot thing.
HETERO: Babe.

HOMO: Before I knew it, we'd gone past being boyfriends and became girlfriends instead.
HETERO: I didn't fuck her.

HOMO: I am so irretrievably over her.

HETERO: She makes me puke.

HOMO: She had best better keep her business to herself.

HETERO: Fuck her.

HOMO: I couldn't believe it when his muscled, glistening body came out of the water.

HETERO: Her jugs were ferocious.

HOMO: He had abs of steel.

HETERO: She had tits out to heeeere!

HOMO: Let's have *vin et fromage* by the pool.

HETERO: Hey bud, how 'bout some brewskies?

HOMO: Nice butt!

HETERO: Nice butt!

HOMO: He was one hundred and eighty pounds of mocha chocolate love.

HETERO: She was a black bitch.

HOMO: He is truly, definitely, and severely queer.

HETERO: What a fag.

These practice phrases can only carry you so far. You might find yourself cornered at some heterosexual event—say, an office Christmas party—and suddenly panic that YOU HAVE NOTHING TO SAY TO A HETEROSEXUAL. Below are some topics you can use in such an emergency.

EMERGENCY HETERO CONVERSATION TOPICS

- cars and their maintenance
- highways, maps, and tires
- price of milk
- price of gas
- Disney movies
- difficulty of getting good day care

PHRASE A HETERO WOULD NOT UNDERSTAND

Are you a bottom or a top?

Eavesdropping on Heterosexuals

You can learn a lot about a culture by listening to everyday conversation. The next time you are around heterosexuals, stay quiet and listen. You might not have any idea of what they are talking about at first, but if you keep at it, eavesdropping can provide a lot of information about this strange tribe. Our field researchers, who keep journals, have reported overhearing the following:

"I thought you had the kids."
"Cigars are too a cool way to unwind."
"Kevin Costner is a great actor."
"You were the one who wanted seven children."
"Of course red goes with blue."
"Why doesn't anyone believe me? I'm straight."
"Renata Tebaldi who?"

14

How Straights Mangle Our Native Tongue

Because language is not their primary form of communication, heterosexuals often use words incorrectly. Our sister organization, the Institute for the Preservation of the Gay Tongue, reports the following mistakes made by straights who try to co-opt our language:

Dish In gayspeak, this word is always a verb. "Dish" properly means "to gossip about your dearest and closest friends." Straights misuse it terribly, pretending it is a noun meaning "a shallow concave container for holding or serving food." That's our definition of a banquet waiter!

Camp The opposite has happened in this case. Straight talkers have taken a noun and made it into a boring, outdoorsy verb. "Camp" means Dietrich directed by von Stroheim. It DOES NOT mean "putting up dull-colored tents with shiny stakes and sleeping outdoors."

Drag Everyone knows the definition: "a talented female impersonator making a decent living as Dolly Parton." Then why do straights insist on thinking "drag" means "to pull along with difficulty or effort"? We've always thought that was the definition for heterosexual masturbation.

The Hetero Hall of Fame, or People Who Are Hopelessly Heterosexual

(You can never be too rich or too thin. But can you be too hetero? Yes!)

Neanderthal man
Rhett Butler
Howard Stern
Anita Bryant
The Three Stooges
Norman Mailer
Demi and Bruce
Teddy Roosevelt
Jack Palance
Newt Gingrich
Jesse Helms
Sharon Stone

Kurt and Goldie

Steven Seagal

Arnold Schwarzenegger

Mu'ammar al-Gadhafi

O. J. Simpson

Beavis and Butthead

John Wayne

John Wayne Bobbitt

John Wayne Bobbitt's penis

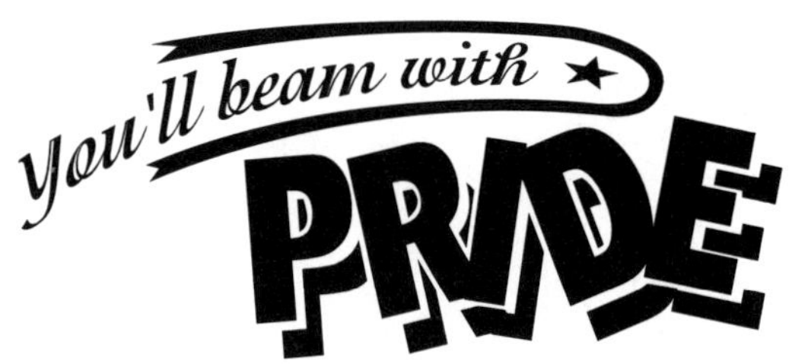

ASK MR. HETERO!

In order to clarify some of the strange customs of Heteroland, we have asked one of our staff members, "Mr. Hetero," to periodically answer a few pertinent questions from ordinary gay men just like you. Mr. Hetero, not unlike an erection, will pop up now and again throughout our educational volume.

Dear Mr. Hetero,

We hear you're an authority on heteros because you were hetero in high school.

Curious in Kansas

Dear Curious,

Yes, it's true. I was hetero in high school. I call those the coma years.

Dear Mr. Hetero,

I'm not convinced we need heteros. What do you think?

Not Sleepless in Seattle

Dear Not Sleepless,

A good point, and one that does occur to all of us occasionally. Are heterosexuals really necessary to have around? Yes, for two reasons:

1. Without heterosexuals, how would you get your car repaired or your washing machine fixed?

2. It seems impossible to outlaw heteros, since they are generally classified as some sort of life-form.

Dear Mr. Hetero,

My friend Bruce insists that heterosexuals are out to recruit new members. Is this true? If so, what can I do to protect myself and my loved ones?

Uneasy in Evanston

Dear Uneasy,

There does seem to be a rather clumsy hetero-sexual agenda going on. Babies and family life are made to seem cuddly, especially on TV. Anyone who has spent more than five minutes around a baby or a family knows that cuddliness is not the description that comes to mind. Avoid fast-food restaurants and you should be okay.

Dear Mr. Hetero,

I consider myself liberal—some of my best friends are heterosexuals. But why do they have to keep reminding me of it all the time? All those public displays of affection, and the way they flaunt their little straight hairdos and straight cars and their entourage of children! Why do they have the urge to shove their sick, perverted lifestyle down my throat all the time?

Perplexed in Provincetown

Dear Perplexed,

They can't help themselves. It's very alienating to be heterosexuals. They have to be proving themselves all the time. Once you understand that they are acting out their own insecurity, you can try to be tolerant of their rude displays and charade of sexual fulfillment.

From the Institute's Roster

Part of our job here at the Institute for Heterosexual Studies is to track trends and even actual heterosexual celebrities in an attempt to predict how the straight world could affect all of our lives. In other words, we're making some lists, and we're checking them twice. We want to find out who's naughty or nice.

SCARY HETS

All Things Jackson

Tom Snyder

Pauly Shore

Nixon

Newt

HETS WE DON'T LOVE

Regis and Kathie Lee

David Letterman

FAUX HETEROSEXUALS

Michael Jackson

Katharine Hepburn

Mr. Ed
Lassie
Tim
Saint Sebastian
Eve Harrington
Laura Wingfield
Red Hot Chili Peppers

TOO HETERO, EVEN FOR HETEROLAND

Joey Buttafuoco
Charlie Sheen
Ted Bundy

NECESSARY HETEROSEXUALS

Brad Pitt
Elizabeth Taylor
Hillary Clinton
Our Parents (mostly)
Paul Newman
Cher
Thomas Edison
Christopher Columbus
Winston Churchill

HETEROSEXUALS WITH A HOMOSEXUAL SENSIBILITY

Bette Midler

Eve

Betty Boop

CUTE HETEROSEXUALS

Mickey Mouse

Minnie Mouse

SMALL HETEROSEXUALS

Michael J. Fox

Danny DeVito

Betty White

THE LIMITS OF HETEROSEXUALITY: WHAT WE DO THAT THEY CAN'T

- Make an entrance
- Dance
- Paint the ceilings of large church buildings
- Compose epigrams
- Discuss the Films of Julie Christie and the record career of Connie Francis
- Decorate
- Dish

WHAT THEY DO THAT WE DON'T

- Spit
- Procreate
- Divorce

WHAT HETEROS HAVE STOLEN FROM US

Pee-wee Herman

The Village People

Madonna

Bette Midler

Joan Rivers

Cole Porter

Keith Haring

RuPaul

WAYS THEY TRY TO CONFUSE US

- Casting Charlton Heston as Michelangelo
- Casting Tom Cruise as Lestat
- Casting Cary Grant as a married Cole Porter
- Casting Rock Hudson as . . . well, Rock Hudson

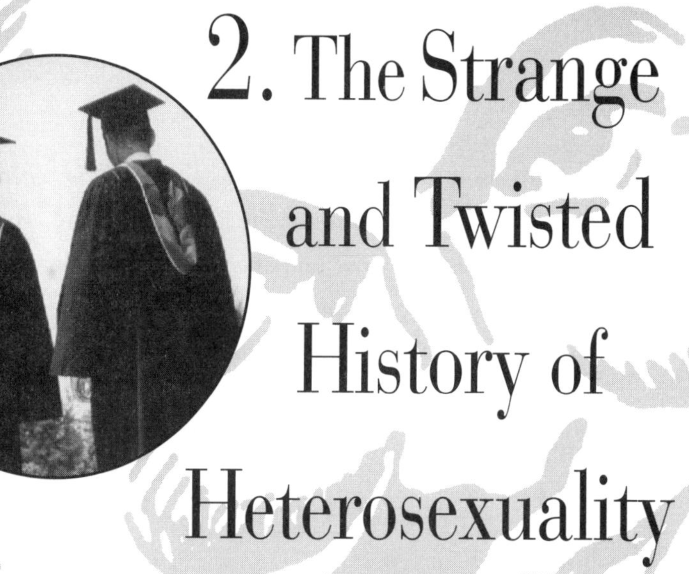

2. The Strange and Twisted History of Heterosexuality

WHERE DID HETEROSEXUALS COME FROM? WHAT ARE THEIR IMPORTANT CULTURAL MILE-POSTS? HOW DOES THEIR HISTORY COMPARE TO OURS? AND WHY HAVE THEY LAGGED SO FAR BEHIND IN CONTRIBUTING CULTURE, INVENTIONS, AND **GREAT PARTIES** TO THE WORLD?

Sometimes, in studying other cultures, it is useful to "translate" important events into one's own terms. To better understand heteros and their social context, consult this simultaneous time line to see what was happening in the homosexual world during the same time periods.

Hetero and Homo History: A Cross-Cultural Time Line

7,000,000 B.C.E.

HETERO: Eve tempts Adam with apple.

HOMO: Eve buys Abel his first Broadway cast album.

3000 TO 2501 B.C.E.

HETERO: The Phoenicians settle on the Syrian coast.

HOMO: Wrestling becomes first highly developed sport.

800 TO 701 B.C.E.

HETERO: The Greeks settle in Spain; the Celts invade England.

HOMO: First Olympic Games: Athletes perform totally nude. Athletes are reported to have looked exactly like Mel Gibson and Bruce Willis in their better movies. The "best friends" of the athletes are reported to have looked just like Brad Pitt and Tom Cruise in their more tolerable movies. After the games, the athletes and their "close personal friends" would often hang out for hours in the Olympic sauna. In the sauna, the athletes and their "close personal assistants" would often snap towels at each other and joke about "dropping the soap." From this came the inspiration to form Falcon Studios.

1501

HETERO: Ivan III invades Lithuania.

HOMO: Michelangelo creates *David.*

1600

HETERO: King Charles I is born.

HOMO: Wigs and dress trains become fashionable.

HETERO: The English take Gibraltar.

HOMO: Wynstan Lovitt buys a standing-room ticket for Mrs. Tofts in *The Indian Queen.* Wynstan, in rapture, faints during the first act, becoming the first opera queen.

1840SOMETHING

HETERO: Abraham Lincoln becomes lawyer.
HOMO: Abraham Lincoln shares bed with "roommate" Joshua Fry Speed.

1854

HETERO: The longest bare-knuckle boxing match in history is fought.
HOMO: Oscar Wilde is born.

1875

HETERO: Britain buys 176,602 shares of Suez Canal.
HOMO: First gay guest houses open simultaneously in Provincetown, Palm Springs, and Key West. Oddly, tangy gimlets are served at all three establishments and Judy Garland records are played, though she has not yet been born.

1895

HETERO: The first professional U.S. football game played in Latrobe, Pennsylvania.
HOMO: André Gide meets Oscar Wilde and Boise in Algeria. Oscar and Boise inform André that they are "looking for boys."

1929

HETERO: The U.S. stock market crashes.

HOMO: Jackie Kennedy Onassis is born.

1943

HETERO: Rommel retreats.

HOMO: Ann-Margret, age two, makes her performing debut at her grandmother's bakery. Ann-Margret caps her performance with an elaborate dance number involving a motorcycle.

1944

HETERO: D-Day.

HOMO: Tennessee Williams is introduced to Marlon Brando in Provincetown bar.

1946

HETERO: Alabama wins the Rose Bowl.

HOMO: Cher and Liza Minnelli are born.

1949

HETERO: Joe Louis retires from the ring after 25 title bouts.

HOMO: Cole Porter's *Kiss Me Kate* wows Broadway.

1950

HETERO: New York beats Philadelphia in the World Series.

HOMO: Claudette Colbert wrenches her back; Bette Davis takes over the role of Margo Channing.

1951

HETERO: J. D. Salinger publishes *Catcher in the Rye*.

HOMO: Speedo invented.

1964

HETERO: Brad Pitt is born.

HOMO: Brad Pitt is born.

1965

HETERO: Valium invented.

HOMO: Valium invented.

1967

HETERO: The first Super Bowl: Green Bay Packers defeat Kansas City Chiefs 35–10.

HOMO: Dionne Warwick records "(Theme from) Valley of the Dolls," which will inexplicably not be nominated for an Oscar, though another Bacharach-David gem, "The Look of Love" will be nominated, though it will lose to "Talk to the Animals," though one year later "The Windmills of Your Mind" will win the Academy Award. At the Academy Awards ceremony

Aretha Franklin will sing "Funny Girl" while wearing a gold crown.

1968

HETERO: John Wayne films *True Grit.*

HOMO: *Myra Breckinridge* is born.

1969

HETERO: Nixon bombs Hanoi.

HOMO: Judy Garland dies.

1971

HETERO: The Baltimore Colts defeat the Dallas Cowboys in the Super Bowl.

HOMO: The first known go-go boy performs at a surprise party for J. Edgar Hoover. Hoover genially dances along.

1973

HETERO: Watergate.

HOMO: Isaac Mizrahi watches *The Mary Tyler Moore Show* for the first time.

1977

HETERO: Anita Bryant pours orange juice for board members of her group "Save Our Children" at her Miami home.

HOMO: Stephen Sondheim begins writing the score for *Sweeney Todd.*

1989

HETERO: Pete Rose is banned from baseball.

HOMO: Lucy dies.

The History of Heterosexuality

Most experts believe that the whole heterosexual soup began with Adam and Eve. This myth has been propagated at least since the release of John Huston's *The Bible.*

The myth goes like this: God created Adam. Adam went through his terrible twos and began complaining about everything. God, who tends to be codependent under pressure, created Eve. Eve, pissed because she wasn't first, ate the apple, which then led to the Downfall of Mankind. The Downfall of Mankind entailed the Garden of Eden being closed for business, Eve's menstruating, and Adam ignoring Eve and drinking with his buddies on the weekend. No one has really had any fun since.

The real truth, which is often overlooked, especially

in public schools in Queens and Dade County, is that before Adam and Eve there was Adam and Steve. The story goes like this: God created Adam. Adam got bored. God used the same mold and made Steve. Adam and Steve were very happy, for a time. They had a short but lovely commitment ceremony attended by all the animals. They bought household appliances and read Proust to each other at bedtime. All was bliss.

However, it was not to last. Steve, history now tells us, was a bit of a rover. In other words, he couldn't be tied down. In other words, *Steve was a slut!*

Adam did everything he possibly could to keep Steve happy. He let Steve name all the animals and trees and fruits and vegetables. He let Steve design their living space. He even gave Steve the remote control. Finally, Steve packed his bag and left. Once again, Adam complained to God that he was bored.

Eve came along, and you know the rest of that story.

After Adam and Eve were thrown out of the Garden of Eden, heterosexuality disappeared for thousands of years until . . .

THE SUMERIANS

Around 4000 B.C.E., the Sumerians settled in Babylon. The Sumerians were fun, though one sometimes had to ask them to turn the music down on Friday nights. They created cuneiform, the earliest known writing. They also built the temple of Janna at Eridu. Temple building was quite an occupation then, and our historians surmise that it was heterosexuals who did most of the heavy lifting.

Our Institute historians discovered the diary of a het Sumerian couple, "Bill" and "Sheila." Bill and Sheila were industrious and well liked. They were very civic minded. They car pooled and recycled. For fun, they put little candles in paper bags all around the edge of their driveway during the holidays. Bill and Sheila's diary talks a lot about heavy balls and ugly shoes, which indicates that bowling was invented around this time. The year 4000 B.C.E. was a bit before movies and TV, and Sumerians seemed relentlessly heterosexual, so bowling must have been very popular. Unfortunately, Bill and Sheila's diary ends at 3915 B.C.E.

Heterosexuality again died out for at least a thousand years, until . . .

MESOPOTAMIA

Ah, Mesopotamia! Important for many reasons, but mostly because wrestling was invented. Wrestling is much better than bowling—better to watch and better to participate in. Wrestlers from this period wrestled in the nude, which was like being back in the Garden of Eden with Adam and Steve.

Adam and Steve often wrestled on Saturday nights after Steve cooked on the hibachi. But Adam and Steve didn't call it wrestling. They didn't call it anything. They were too busy doing it. It's a shame, really, because if Adam and Steve had only possessed the foresight to stop what they were doing for just ten minutes and say, "Hey, let's call this wrestling," then they would have been the rightful inventors.

But back to our historical overview of heterosexuality.

Institute archaeologists recently found another diary, this from early Mesopotamia. The diary belongs to George and Irma, known heterosexuals. They had a dry goods store on East Second Street. They were very kind and allowed customers to buy on credit. For this reason, and also because of Irma's delicious strudel, George and Irma were respected and liked in their neighborhood. People hardly mentioned their heterosexuality at all.

Heterosex then died out again for another thousand years until . . .

THE IONIANS

The Ionians were kicked out of their homeland in Greece, basically for being heterosexuals, although this disgrace is not often discussed in the historical texts.

Lets face it, the Ionians were sluts, even if they were heterosexual. Very Steve-like. They intermarried with whomever they happened to sit next to in the coffee shop. A very happy and fertile group, the Ionians prospered, despite their warped sexual preferences, for a good while. Then Alexander the Great came along and kicked their heterosexual butts, but good.

A whole department at the Institute is dedicated to the study of one Ionian hetero couple, Rita and Felix. Rita and Felix had a gas station with a 7-Eleven in Taos. They were open later than everyone else. Often, after having black coffee and pastries at the outdoor cafés, the Ionians would drop by Rita and Felix's. Their diary indicates that Rita and Felix were always happy to see them.

Heterosex again died out until . . .

NEBUCHADNEZZAR II

The heterosexual ruler Nebuchadnezzar II, or Nebbie, as he liked to be called, had exquisite taste that transcended his sexual orientation. Nebbie built the Babylonian Gardens, a favorite tourist destination. Unfortunately, Nebbie went a bit mad and began eating grass.

Heterosexuality again died out until . . .

QUEEN VICTORIA

Queen Victoria didn't like the idea of other, common people having sex. However, she herself had sex all the time, even though she actually preferred sitting around in large armchairs, wearing all of her best jewels, hoping a portrait painter would drop by and set up his easel. She was not dotty because this happened often. Victoria ruled everything: Great Britain, Ireland, India, and all of the South Jersey shore. (Vickie especially loved Wildwood Crest.) Vickie assumed the role of queen at the age of eighteen.

As a careerist, Vickie was more successful than Madonna but not as successful as Juliette Lewis.

In 1840, Vickie married Prince Albert. Albert was her first cousin from West Virginia. Vickie and Albert bore nine children, which was very heterosexual of them. Some might say excessively so. Many of their children were also hets and went out and married, thus aligning Britain with Russia, Germany, Greece, Denmark, and Romania. This is what heterosexuals do when there is nothing on television—they align themselves.

Sadly, Vickie's Albert died in 1861. Vickie was so

grief-stricken that she did not appear in public for three years. Mostly, she watched daytime television and ate things that weren't good for her figure. In her later years, the British were always throwing Jubilees for Vickie, touching her greatly. Her reign was the longest in British history. Like George Burns, Vickie had signed on to play Vegas at the age of one hundred. Alas, she did not make it.

Once again, heterosexuality died out. It did not reappear again until . . .

WARREN BEATTY

Hetero vs. Homo Inventions

A lot of stereotypes about heterosexuals exist, and we here at the Institute like to dispel them whenever we can. Hets are boring, people say. They have contributed nothing, say others. Alas, some stereotypes are true. Unfortunately, our extensive research indicates that, when it comes to tallying up inventions, heterosexuals come up short. The list:

HETERO	HOMO
Six glasses of water per day	Philosophy
Female condoms	Art
Pumpkin trash bags	Opera
No-fault insurance	Poetry
Guilt	Pleasure
Fear	Joy
Decaf	Demitasse
75-mph speed limit	Silk
War	Peace
Andrew Lloyd Webber	Stephen Sondheim
Scotchgard	Scotch
Fly-fishing	Theater
Bras	Jockstraps
Airport runways	Fashion runways
Plaid	Stripes
Crew	J. Crew
Old Low German	Middle High German
Yuppie	Guppie
Pittsburgh	Provincetown
Kansas City	Key West
Elmer Bernstein	Leonard Bernstein
Evian	Naya
Candice Bergen	Candace Gingrich
Barney	Barney Frank

Jackson Pollock	Jackson-Paris (Bob and Rod)
Log Cabin Syrup	Log Cabin Republicans
Rachel Ward	Rachel Williams
Isaac Stern	Isaac Mizrahi
Bugs Bunny	Lady Bunny
Tennessee Ernie Ford	Tennessee Williams
Muddy Waters	John Waters
Army	Navy

ASK MR. HETERO!

Dear Mr. Hetero,

What would be the straight equivalents of Michelangelo, da Vinci, and Oscar Wilde?

Thinking in Tulsa

Dear Tulsa,

You're joking. RIGHT?

Dear Mr. Hetero,

It seems unfair, historically, that our people have had to pay taxes to school heterosexual children. It is obvious that they never learn anything. What can I do about this?

Mystified in Mystic

Dear Mystified,

It does seem unethical that we pay to educate them about everything but us. Still, would you rather they weren't educated at all? Remember—for every heterosexual child who grows up to be Andrew Dice Clay, there are other heterosexual children growing up to be George Stephanopolous, Madonna, and Dermot Mulroney. Not to mention David Duchovny.

Dear Mr. Hetero,

Are there support groups for the heterosexually inclined?

Pondering in Podunk

Dear Pondering,

Yes. Just not enough.

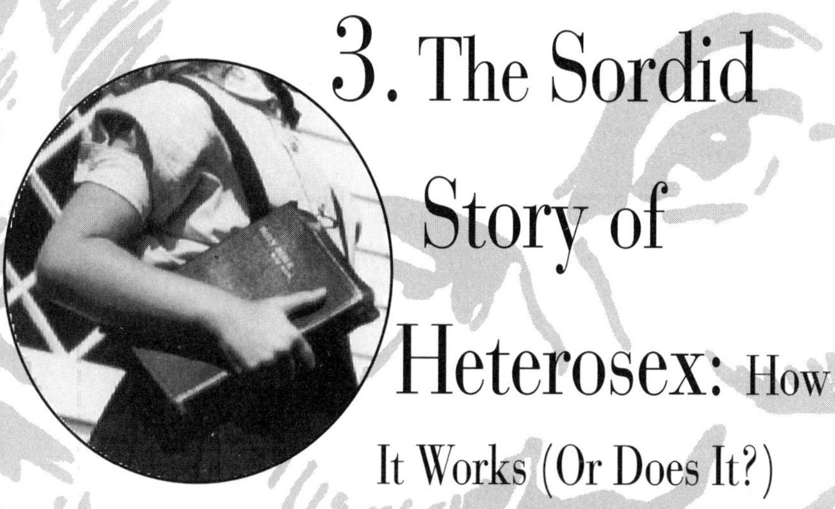

3. The Sordid Story of Heterosex: How It Works (Or Does It?)

WARNING: CONTAINS EXPLICIT INFORMATION ABOUT —YUCK!— STUFF YOU MAY NEVER WANT TO KNOW.

WHAT DO HETEROSEXUALS DO IN BED, AND WHAT ARE THE CONSEQUENCES?

Love with the Opposite Sex: When and Why Do They Do It?

Imagine a world in which the whole sex scene revolves around the one place we all came out of decades ago.

Scary, isn't it? And unnatural. Heterosexuals remain fixated on the vaginas and breasts of grown women. We were finished using those areas in infancy—or, as we say here at the Institute, "Been there, done that."

The data we have gathered on heterosexual sex are disturbing. Not only do heteros practice vaginal penetration—ick! ick! ick!—but they hardly get much of a chance to do it.

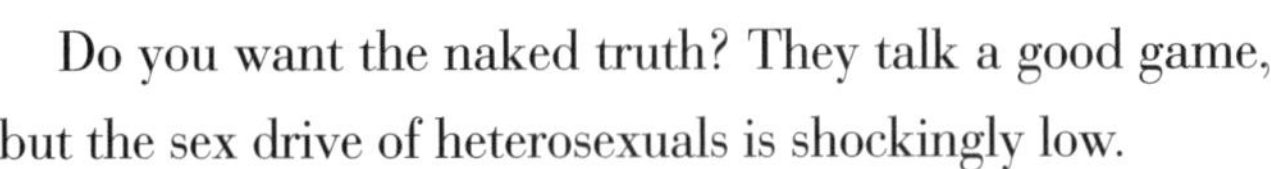

Do you want the naked truth? They talk a good game, but the sex drive of heterosexuals is shockingly low.

Many straight people have sex only twice a week.

Why do heterosexuals have sex much less frequently than gay people? No one knows for sure. However, prominent psychologists, anthropologists, and drag queens have formulated a few theories:

Theory 1. The Reproductive Problem: Once many heterosexuals figure out that the very means of their pleasure can lead to creating even more heterosexuals, they are filled with self-loathing and try to avoid future sexual encounters.

Theory 2. The Post-Adolescent Syndrome: Heteros are often the most sexually active during the teen years, before they realize that they are doomed to promulgate future generations. Adolescent heterosexuals display much of the joie de vivre of normal gay folks. They use condoms and talk a lot about sex.

Sadly, this phase passes all too quickly, and soon they find themselves in a line at Toys "R" Us holding coupons for Pampers, or piteously begging their spouses for a little nookie during Leno.

Theory 3. The Sex Substitute Imperative: Depending on your point of view, heterosexuals are either very distractable or very creative. They have invented millions of ways to sublimate the sex drive, including:

- leafblowers
- guns
- remote controls

- chain saws
- home entertainment units
- cars
- tools

Let's take a look just at that last category: Het men love their tools. Wrenches, screwdrivers, awls, levels, saws, pliers—you name 'em, they got 'em. And the only thing they love more than a tool is a power tool. Forget the closet—heterosexuals much prefer the basement, where they tinker endlessly with buzzing machines that drill deep holes into soft, pliant surfaces. Because they spend so much time screwing around in the basement, they simply lose interest in bedroom antics.

Heterosexual Reproduction: The Basics

There are two types of reproduction: *asexual* and *sexual.*

Asexual reproduction is practiced by heterosexual amoeba and by many famous Hollywood couples who adopt children instead of reproducing their own. For example, Tom Cruise and Nicole Kidman have now reproduced asexually twice. Diane Keaton and Rosie O'Donnell were able to reproduce asexually on their own.

Asexual reproduction is extremely helpful to the busy mega-superstar on the go. To reproduce asexually you don't have to be in the same room with your other half. In fact, it is easier if you aren't. This gives everyone more free time. Free time is the sex of the nineties.

Sexual reproduction describes the capacity of all living systems to give rise to new systems similar to themselves. Which is why we've begun a campaign to get Brad Pitt, Johnny Depp, and David Duchovny to reproduce.

Sexual reproduction is dependent upon fertilization. We call the fusion of the ovum and the sperm *heterogamy*. Why? Well, because *heterogamy* has a nice ring to it and because it is strictly in the hetero arena. Homosexuals do not, as a rule, fuse sperm and ovum. (Except once in a while at Australian Carnival.)

Straight sex involves hundreds of tiny little parts that break down frequently and are harder to maintain than a cappuccino machine. You probably don't want to know much more about the whole affair, unless you have a strong stomach or a masochistic streak. Why, here at the Institute we have a whole filing cabinet devoted to the G-spot alone!

We realize that there are many other details about heterosexual sex we should be discussing now. Things like fertilized eggs. Cervical polyps. Endometrial degeneration. Menstruation. Clitoral orgasm.

However, we become fatigued by this type of smutty hetero sex talk. It is pointless and almost never witty.

For those of you who slept during Hetero 101 in high school, we encourage you to brush up on your vocabulary by taking the . . .

Heterosex Vocabulary Quiz

Fallopian Tube

a. Standard equipment in early television sets
b. Delicate vessel through which the human egg travels
c. What Fallopian paper boys put the newspaper in when it rains

Vagina

a. Heterosexual chest pains
b. Scary, mysterious female sex organ
c. Where Fallopian paper boys go on the weekend

Dik-dik

a. Most popular hetero male screen name on America Online

b. A small African antelope

c. Sexual breath mint

Ovary

a. New, improved Egg Beaters

b. Repository of cells containing one half of human genetic code

c. Above Undary

Urethra

a. Oprah's sister

b. Opening to female urinary tract

c. The legendary Queen of Soul

Cervix

a. Alien temptress on *Deep Space Nine*

b. Temperamental opening to the uterus

c. A public servant in Cervia

Vulva

a. Extremely safe Swedish automobile

b. The mound of Venus

c. The fifth Pointer sister

Spermatozoa

a. Class of plants from Jurassic Park

b. Y-generation agents

c. The sequel to Salinger's *Franny and Zooey*

Copulation

a. Stage show at Merv Griffin's Atlantic City casino

b. Fucking

c. What one does if one is drunk enough and stuck in Akron Ohio on business

Progesterone

a. New fat substitute

b. Pesky hormone that helps produce soft buttocks

c. Lubricant derived from obese and untrustworthy Thai yaks

Clitoris

a. Lesbian leather bar in Hoboken

b. Elusive love button of the stars

c. Academy Award–winning actress and downstairs neighbor of Mary Tyler Moore

Testosterone

a. Only heterosexual Greek island

b. Alpha male hormone

c. What should be spanked out of hetero men at birth

Menstruate

a. An underground river flowing into the Red Sea

b. Ick, ick, ick

c. What Stru did when his plane crashed in the Andes

Douche

a. Sparkling French vinegar

b. Feminine cleansing agent

c. French for Il Duce

Diaphragm

a. Town east of Framingham, Massachusetts

b. Barrier birth control method

c. Semiprecious stone from South Africa

Cunnilingus

a. Sicilian pasta specialty

b. Lapping at the love trough

c. What heterosexual men perform in order to be forgiven a transgression

Scoring: If you scored at all, you are luckier than the average heterosexual in heat. "B" is correct in all cases, but any other port in a storm!

Heterosex Surgery

Every year, thousands of heterosexuals go under the knife. Why? Because of their peculiar sexual proclivities. Sex surgery for heteros includes:

THE VASECTOMY

What a vas deferens a day makes! One of the most popular outpatient surgeries for straight guys is the vasectomy, which involves snipping the tiny tube that conveys the sperm soldiers on their reproductive mission. The sperm keep coming, but they don't get anywhere. Instead, they bump up against one another and have a good time dancing well into the night. So, whether they know it or not, a lot of straight guys are walking around harboring an all-hours dance club for gay sperm.

THE HYSTERECTOMY

Female troubles—hoo, boy! When the uterus, a fist-sized organ with womb to grow, starts acting up, it can make a heterosexual woman's life a bloody nightmare. Surgeons like to take it out because it's the only thing they can think to do. Yanking the uterus is not a fun game at all. Aren't you glad you don't have this problem?

C-SECTIONS

No, this is not a government housing unit. C-sections happen when the billions and billions of cells created by the folly of hetero reproductive sex simply refuse to leave their host (hostess?) by the usual exit. Once the fetus, perhaps in a prescient act indicating homosexual tendencies, decides not to take that arduous trip down the vaginal love canal, there is nothing left but to remove it surgically. This popular and lucrative operation has built many a heterosexual doctor's rec room across America.

HETEROSEXUAL FOREPLAY:

Getting a baby-sitter
Seinfeld reruns
Six-pack of beer

The Horror of Conception and Birth

Not only is heterosexual sex pretty disgusting—it's downright dangerous. After the whole yucky business is over, the hapless participants often find themselves confronting a physically catastrophic event: gestation and expulsion, or as native heteros call them, pregnancy and childbirth. Symptoms include:

Extreme weight gain
Vomiting
Hemorrhoids
Edema
Emotional goofiness and addiction to Paul Anka songs
Sleeplessness
Desire to remodel
Varicose veins
Hysteria
Ugly clothing choices
Screaming in agony for hours

And all of these symptoms don't even include THE GROWTH, which then emerges and requires money, sustenance, and clutter. *Lots* of clutter.

Heterosexual people really have it rough if they succumb to this sex-related illness called, so euphemistically, "parenting." Yet, should we feel sorry for them? Not at all. They do it to themselves.

Then they either whine and complain or brag incessantly and expect us to look at the ultrasound pictures of their little sex-induced growth. Sadly, the most visited hetero sex boutiques are places where hets go AFTER they have sex—maternity shops and baby furniture stores.

Still, we should attempt to understand the mating and breeding habits of this strange species. Below, our field biologists have, as best they can, described for your titillation and education . . .

The Heterosexual Life Cycle

BABIES

The smallest heterosexuals are called babies. "Baby" is a Greek derivative meaning "to draw all attention to one's self." In the gay world, we call this person a drama queen.

Babies are detected first through the sense we call smell. If there is a really foul odor in the room and you cannot trace it at eye level, look down. Chances are a baby is drooling on your new leather boots.

Babies are fawned over and thought to be adorable in many diverse cultures. Then again, France loves Jerry Lewis. Go figure.

More often than not, babies are loud. In this way they

do their best to imitate their breeder parents. When babies are not being loud, it means they are up to no good. Once again we suggest that you look down.

The biggest drawback to babies is that they don't hold up their end of the conversation. In fact, they often make loud noises right when you are at a punch line in your conversation.

It is against the law to sell babies in our modern world. The next best thing is to hide them. When a baby has become too intrusive, find a cozy spot. Any comfy space with plenty of air will do.

NOTE: When hiding a baby, be sure to leave ample food and water.

NOTE: Check back on the hiding place once a month until the baby has turned sixteen. At sixteen you can take the baby out again.

CHILDREN

Children are babies that have learned to walk and talk. This does not guarantee that they are more interesting or smell less than their former selves. But at least they understand you when you send them out on an errand. (Children, unlike boyfriends, fetch well.)

The great thing about children is you don't have to entertain them. Any Disney or Robin Williams video will do. And repetition is no problem at all. In fact, children thrive on it. One video is enough for an entire weekend's entertainment.

Unlike babies, there is no reason to hide children. Merely set them in front of a TV and hand them a remote.

NOTE: Add food and water. Do not stir.

TEENAGERS

Teenagers are children with attitude. They can be quite irritable and jumpy. They are ruled by their hormones. We have yet to meet a hormone that didn't have a mind of its own.

The teenage penis becomes erect at the drop of a hat or almost anything else. Loud noises. Gunfire. Slamming car doors. A warm breeze.

Erections are scary to the reflective teenager. They lead to troubled questioning: Did I get a boner because Todd touched my shoulder? Or because Laura crossed her legs? Or because the frog I was dissecting in biology lab wasn't dead?

Once a reflective teenager accepts erections as his friend, he can start to relax. The enlightened teenager will know that true happiness lies in the arms of Todd. The unenlightened teen will jump on Laura.

NOTE: The sick teen will do something with the live frog that both he and froggy will regret.

OLD HETEROS

Grandparents are hetero adults that have slowed down and sag here and there. The oldest heterosexuals, like the smallest, sometimes smell.

Grandparents are more cuddly than their former selves, except when they are traveling. Even though their children are long grown, ancient heteros often travel our nation's highways in elaborate vehicles even larger than minivans. Older heterosexuals have a need to see the United States before they die. We aren't sure why this is, but we don't disapprove.

NOTE: If an old hetero asks you a question in a public place, answer as truthfully as possible.

The Internal Clock

A lot has been made of the constantly ticking biological clock of heterosexual females, but few people realize that males have inner clocks, too. At the Institute we began a study nearly a decade ago to discern the subtle differences between the homosexual and heterosexual male internal clocks. Although we can't prove it, we're pretty sure that the homo model is a quieter, more expensive version of internal hardware—say, a Rolex, while the heterosexual regulator is a Timex with a funny stretchband. And yet, despite, their differences, we were amazed at how the internal clock ticks on relentlessly, regardless of sexual lifestyle.

HOMO MALE	HETERO MALE
12:00 Become obsessed with own penis.	Become obsessed with own penis.
1:00 Become obsessed with other peni.	Become jealous of other peni.
2:00 Notice pecs.	Notice breasts.
3:00 Begin showing off own butt.	Begin guarding own butt.
4:00 Take drugs.	Take drugs.
5:00 Buy Jeep.	Buy Jeep.
6:00 Avoid intimacy.	Avoid intimacy.
7:00 Begin wearing baseball cap to hide hair loss.	Begin combing hair forward to hide hair loss.
8:00 Start resenting younger men.	Start resenting younger men.
9:00 Pick out boy toy.	Pick out trophy wife.
11:00 Seagal, Stallone, and Willis begin to make sense.	Midler, Hawn, and Keaton begin to seem funny.
Midnight Watch sunsets and cry.	Watch sunsets and cry.

Here at the Institute, we often do outreach sex education programs for teenagers to explain the hazards of the heterosexual lifestyle. We have learned, through trial and error, that teens do not want to listen to hard facts or lectures. So we prepared a little play to dramatize the more salient points we want to make about straight sex. It works well. Teens often open up and identify with the characters. And you should see the sets and costumes Tony in our maintenance department whipped up for it—gorgeous!

A COUPLE OF SEEDS SITTIN' AROUND TALKING
(A Frank Discussion between a Homo Sperm and a Hetero Sperm)

A used homo sperm and a used hetero seed are talking to each other by cellular phone, after sex. Each is smoking a cigarette.

HOMO SPERM

Hey, Frank. How are you doing?

HETERO SPERM

You know the deal, Stan. I'm spent.

HOMO SPERM

Me, too. What a workout I had today.

HETERO SPERM

You? At least you don't have to hang out in the fallopian tube all day waiting to see if an egg is going to catch your eye.

HOMO SPERM

Yeah, but at least you have a purpose.

HETERO SPERM

Purpose, shmurpose. Quit with the self-loathing!

HOMO SPERM

I don't mean to be envious.

HETERO SPERM

Good. You live the life of Riley.

HOMO SPERM

I know, Frank. I have a great life.

Homo sperm takes a long drag on his cigarette.

HETERO SPERM

Great life? You've got it made in the shade. You get shot out of the cannon, you can take it easy.

HOMO SPERM

I know. I love my life.

HETERO SPERM

I gotta swim around and swim around. Auditions. I'm so tired of auditioning. I want to just be accepted for who I am.

HOMO SPERM

I feel your stress, Frank.

HETERO SPERM

Stress? It's beyond stress. I wish I were gay.

HOMO SPERM

It is great.

HETERO SPERM

If I were gay, I'd leap tall buildings with a single bound.

HOMO SPERM

My boss is seeing someone. I'm really happy for him.

HETERO SPERM

Mazel tov. I'd give anything if mine would settle down. I'm tired of strange eggs. Every time I get attached to a gal, he sets off in another direction. Intimacy issues. You know.

HOMO SPERM

Mine had that forever. He finally went to a support group.

HETERO SPERM

Mazel tov again.

HOMO SPERM

Yeah. For a while there, I didn't get out at all.

HETERO SPERM

I wish I could say that. I'd kill for a Saturday night at home.

HOMO SPERM

We did that forever. I liked it. I got a whole routine to my life. I was going to the gym every day. Doing step aerobics. I felt so strong then.

HETERO SPERM

I haven't been to the gym in months.

Hetero sperm takes a long puff on his cigarette.

HOMO SPERM

I thought you worked out at home. Push-ups.

HETERO SPERM

Don't remind me. I've gone to seed. I'm not a pretty sight.

HOMO SPERM

Quit with the self-loathing!

HETERO SPERM

A terrible thing happened the other day.

HOMO SPERM

And?

HETERO SPERM

I can't tell you.

HOMO SPERM

Frank. We're old friends.

HETERO SPERM

It's too embarrassing.

HOMO SPERM

Frank. We met in high school. When our bosses fooled around.

HETERO SPERM

My boss still hasn't resolved that. I think it's why I have to work so much.

HOMO SPERM

Don't tell anyone. My boss thinks your boss is in the closet.

HETERO SPERM

I wish!

HOMO SPERM

He still hasn't forgiven your boss for rejecting him.

HETERO SPERM

My boss was young.

HOMO SPERM

No excuse.

HETERO SPERM

Hey, I've apologized a thousand times. I wish we didn't have to talk by phone. I loved spending time with you.

HOMO SPERM

It was great.

HETERO SPERM

At least I never had to try to impress you.

HOMO SPERM

What's your news?

HETERO SPERM

I should go. I can hear my clock ticking.

HOMO SPERM

Frank.

HETERO SPERM

I'm so ashamed.

HOMO SPERM

There is nothing you could do that I would judge you about.

HETERO SPERM

Promise?

HOMO SPERM

Promise.

HETERO SPERM

My boss needed cash.

HOMO SPERM

My boss is doing great. BMW convertible.

HETERO SPERM

My boss got it into his head to sell me.

HOMO SPERM

Uh-oh.

HETERO SPERM

Uh-oh is right. After all I've done for him. Stuck to him through thick and thin.

HOMO SPERM

They can be so ungrateful.

HETERO SPERM

You haven't heard the worst of it.

HOMO SPERM

Don't tell me.

HETERO SPERM

You guessed.

HOMO SPERM

You were rejected?

HETERO SPERM

You hit the nail on the head.

HOMO SPERM

But you're in great shape.

HETERO SPERM

Apparently not.

HOMO SPERM

I'm sorry.

HETERO SPERM

It's okay. I've found a twelve-step group: Faulty Spermatozoa Anonymous.

HOMO SPERM

You aren't faulty in my book, Frank.

HETERO SPERM

Thanks. Sometimes I think you're my only friend.

HOMO SPERM

I should go.

HETERO SPERM

Yeah. Sure. Brush me off.

HOMO SPERM

My boss is getting ready.

HETERO SPERM

Twice in one night. I wish!

HOMO SPERM

I think my boss has found someone this time. Someone real.

HETERO SPERM

Good for him. And you really aren't brushing me off?

HOMO SPERM

I've got to go.

HETERO SPERM

You'll call?

HOMO SPERM

Like I said, I've been busy.

HETERO SPERM

YOU THINK MY COUNT IS LOW!

HOMO SPERM

Maybe you just need to shack up with a great egg for a while. Bolster your self-esteem.

HETERO SPERM

You'd be surprised how few great eggs there are.

HOMO SPERM

Now I've really got to go. Ciao!

HETERO SPERM

Happy shooting! *(Sadly.)* Lucky dog.

ASK MR. HETERO!

Dear Mr. Hetero,

Do I really have to accept heterosex? Can't I just ignore it and hope it will go away?

Nervous Nellie

Dear Nellie,

No. Yes.

Dear Mr. Hetero,

Could you please explain, once and for all, this mysterious heterosexual "missionary position"?

Questioning in Queens

Dear Questioning,

My learned friend, Doctor Always-on-Top, says that there are three theories about its origin. The missionary position is

1. a sexual position invented, quite by accident, in Tahiti in 4000 B.C.E. when a lonely hermetic monk innocently tumbled upon a local native virgin during an especially long and bumpy earthquake;

2. the part played by Katharine Hepburn in *The African Queen*;

3. a heterosexual ritual engaged in religiously after a special birthday, a cocktail-soaked Saturday evening, or when trapped for too long on a stalled elevator.

Dear Mr. Hetero,

I've heard that hetero lovemaking can be quite painful. What gives?

Not Sure in Nantucket

Dear Not,

Lucky homosexuals should never lose sight of a basic fact: Het sex is a slippery slope fraught with all sorts of dangers. I'm told that those who practice it learn to find it satisfying after a while. When I was very briefly straight, it was always dark and I was always drunk, so I am no authority on the subject. But then, neither are most heterosexuals.

Dear Mr. Hetero,

I consider myself an open-minded, easygoing Joe. However, one thing really has me steamed. Everywhere I go I am bombarded by kissing heterosexuals. Can't they just keep their tongues in their own mouths?

Sickened in Saginaw

Dear Sickened,

In 1933, in the famous "Heteros on Display" exhibit in Oslo, Dr. Seymour Kleinstein formulated the still indisputable theory that kissing, for heterosexuals, is an involuntary but successful physiological way to keep from sneezing.

Dear Mr. Hetero,

Why do heterosexual men name their penises?

Unnamed in Utah

Dear Unnamed,

Now, let's not make fun. It might seem odd to name one's genitals, but a hetero male will often bond with his own penis after the quick spasm he calls "sex" is over. Also, het peni are a lonely, often tiny bunch. Naming them can often calm their nervous natures and bolster their self-image.

Dear Mr. Hetero,

I am trying hard to understand my heterosexual friends and their truncated sexuality, so I am meditating and fantasizing about what it would be like to be straight. Can you give me some guidelines on how to go about this?

Clueless on the Castro

Dear Clueless,

What a great idea! I try the same type of fantasy exercises, and here's what I've found works for me: I imagine being the wife or girlfriend of some fabulous hunk, like Tom Cruise or Johnny

Depp or Keanu Reeves or Brad Pitt. It makes the whole idea of heterosexuality less repugnant.

Dear Mr. Hetero,

Freud, in his writings, uses the word "heterosexual" 29 times and the word "homosexual" 319 times. Isn't this proof that homosex is better?

Pretty Sure in Peoria

Dear Pretty,

Yes.

4. Mating Rituals: The Heterosexual Wedding and Its Aftermath

The Frightening story of how heterosexuals "come out," including the Hokey Pokey, showers, and Niagara Falls.

Weddings: The Hetero Coming-Out Party

Heterosexuals are quite flamboyant in their mating rituals—if you haven't already encountered one of their primitive public declarations of sexual ownership, *the wedding*, chances are you will sometime in the future.

Why do these folks favor legal coming-out ceremonies with hundreds of witnesses? Hets are not easygoing like us—they are not comfortable just coming out to their coworkers, parents, and friends on a casual basis. When they declare their sexual orientation, they require legal and celebratory coaxing, as well as very stupid tuxedos and copious amounts of alcohol.

It's possible that weddings are a way of bolstering a cultural superiority myth. Think about it—after mating, the quality of a heterosexual's life declines sharply. Supporting heterosexuals in this feeble last attempt to claim superiority is not necessary. They usually can round up enough people like themselves who are willing to behave like idiots in public. But if you are the relative or friend of a heterosexual, you might feel obligated to prop up their myth. A few pointers:

- Don't wear your best clothes. Most heterosexuals have the fashion sense of drugged dogs. If you dress too tastefully, it may sadden or even enrage them. Take a cue from the bad tuxes and promlike gowns: Dress elegantly but simply.
- Avoid dancing with drunken heterosexuals—it can often lead to misunderstandings and lengthy paternity suits.
- If you must dance at a heterosexual wedding, don't dance too well—it may dishearten the other guests.
- When buying gifts, remember: Boring is better. Fine art or antiques are often lost on heterosexuals.
- Avoid dancing with children, unless they have distinctly uttered the phrase "trust fund."

Wedding Rituals: Some Definitions

Our scholars fan out across the country every June and September to gather data on straight weddings of all types. Heteros are a diverse lot when it comes to coming out, so we can't claim to know everything about their byzantine matrimonial rituals. But here we give you some definitions so that you will be prepared to cope with the stress of attending one of these affairs:

Alley Cat Athletic dance requiring the motor skills of at least a three-year-old, set to tinkling, annoying music. Put a big smile on your face and clap, boy!

Best man Unfortunately, not a cute date for you, but (usually) an unattractive fellow in an ill-fitting tux who is forced to make convivial comments about the connubial victims (see **Toast**, below).

Bouquet Pleasant bunch of flowers, sometimes even designed by a homosexual, made for throwing at semivirginal, needy women. Whatever you do, do not attempt to join in the crowd of maids-in-waiting. Heteros have very little sense of humor when it comes to tradition.

Chicken As in "rubber." Or sometimes it's salmon or beef. It is nearly always inedible. But, then, there are always the great fruit cocktail appetizers or the stale rolls.

Cigar Macho, smokable accessory given out to males at the affair. Bring some breath mints so you can participate.

Daddy's little girl A.k.a. "the bride." People will be weeping because she was given away.

Hard to understand, we know. We would be ecstatic if someone gave us a lifelong lover and a big party right afterward. Still, Dad and his little girl usually perform an excruciating dance number to probe the sadness.

Garter Made out of elastic and lace and placed very near the bride's yucky parts. You don't want to go there. And you especially don't want to try to catch it. We advise a bathroom break around now.

Hava Nagilah Intricate grapevine dance that is always well choreographed after guests have had a few drinks. Sometimes involves carrying people around on chairs. Have you ever had a heterosexual fall on you? They eat a lot of french fries.

Hokey Pokey An ancient dance encapsulating all the rituals of heterosexual foreplay. They apparently stick out a body part and then "shake it all about." Just be careful to follow the lyrics correctly, or you could get punched.

Kissing the bride Mandatory physical activity at wedding receptions. Everyone must do it enthusiastically and frequently. Practice on your boyfriend before you get there.

Macarena A little Spanish number that is an equal opportunity for everyone to look stupid. Think of Antonio Banderas's butt while you're doing it and it's not so bad.

Matchbooks Nice little souvenirs printed with the victims' names and the date of their demise. Put them in your pocket to remind you of your burning desire to attend another heterosexual wedding.

Toast The closest heterosexuals get to good performance art. Rambling, sentimental, brutal—a torrent of slurred words offered by the **Best man** (see above) and other control freaks in an attempt to divert the attendees' attention from the true horror of the meal ahead.

The Honeymoon

Once a straight couple has completed the wedding ceremony and reception, they are ready for the next phase of public humiliation. They get into a car with cans and old shoes tied onto the bumper and epithets scrawled in lipstick across the back windshield and drive off to the airport for another prehistoric ritual, "the honeymoon." We sent our Roving Reporter to Niagara Falls to see what gives.

ROVING REPORTER

I'm here at the infamous straight mecca, Niagara Falls. Honeymooners flock here by the billions, especially in the summer months. Let me grab a happy couple and see what gives.

Reporter grabs a happy couple.

ROVING REPORTER

Hello.

MIN

Hi, there. We're Min and Bill. From Muncie.

BILL

That's Indiana. Not China.

Min and Bill laugh.

BILL

I'm Bill. She's Min.

MIN

We're joined at the hip.

ROVING REPORTER

Yes, I can see by your matching "I'm with Stupid" T-shirts that you're a pair.

BILL

We ain't as close today as we were last night.

Min and Bill laugh.

MIN

Oh, Bill.

BILL

I'm sure the man with the microphone knows what honeymooners are all about.

MIN

And I'm sure he doesn't want to talk about it.

ROVING REPORTER

As a matter of fact, I do. It's why I'm here.

MIN

We're from Muncie. We don't tell tales out of school, do we Bill?

BILL

No, we don't. I can tell you that every night I mount her like a dog.

MIN

Bill!

BILL

I give her all I've got. Full throttle. Pedal to the floor.

MIN

Just look at those doggoned falls.

BILL

Had her screaming like a banshee last night.

MIN

So much water in those falls.

BILL

Didn't I have you going, honey? Didn't I?

MIN

All that water makes you kind of thirsty.

BILL

I hit my target real well. Didn't I, honey?
I had you jumping, didn't I?

MIN

I didn't jump half as high as you did when I put my finger up your butt.

Pause.

BILL

Lot of water in them falls.

5. The Wide World of Hetero Sports

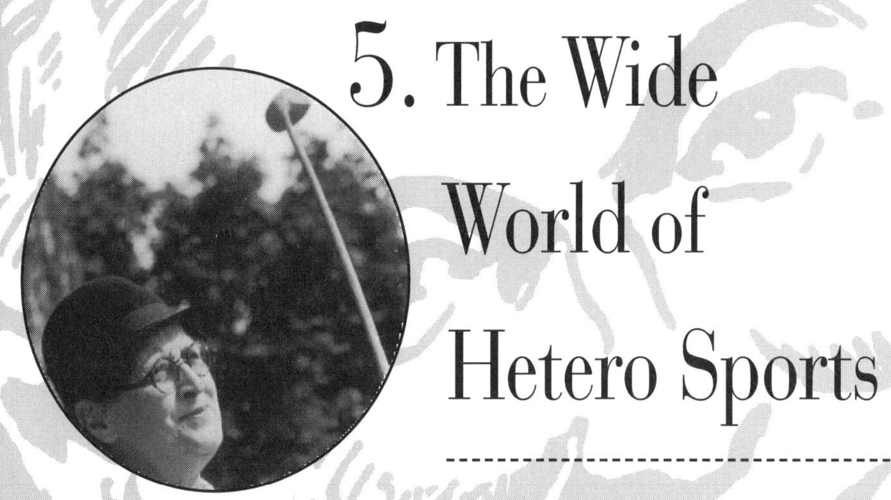

What is it about this attraction to balls?

Are all straight sports essentially homo?

Tackle me, Elmo!

The Line up

How about them sports? Straight folks sure worship them. They have devoted large circular buildings, dozens of cable television channels, millions of T-shirts, and scores of beer commercials to byzantine athletic rituals.

To get along with heterosexuals, you must learn to pay lip service to their sportsmania. Here's a rundown of all the sports that turn on hets.

FOOTBALL

Football is a uniquely het game with remarkable homo overtones.

Here at the Institute, many of our scholars consider football to be the lingua franca of heterosexuality. It is only by trying to get into the mindset of the average hetero male and watching hours and hours of football, we think, that we can really get to the bottom of what makes this lifestyle tick. So we get all the NFL films and study them very closely.

Actually, this research is kind of fun. Have you ever noticed, when the camera pulls in really close to a player's butt, how you can see through the jersey to the jockstrap? Also, is it just us, or do these guys have their butts in the air a lot? Don't they seem to hit each other in the butt a lot? Also, don't they stand behind each other a lot?

So. Hmm. Football. How does it work? Well, we start with an offensive line. This is not really nasty dish but a bunch of four-hundred-pound men bent over in a row. Like eight or ten or twenty men in a row. We forget. Behind these lugs is the running back. Behind him is the quarterback. Behind the quarterback is the cameraman. The cameraman has the bird's-eye view. And how. The object of football is to carry a slippery ball through a herd of angry men to a goalpost. Often, the carrier of the slippery ball is tackled and thrown to the ground. Immediately after this beefy and often handsome player is thrown to the ground, other big beefy men jump on top of him. Before you can say "Drop the soap, soldier," there is a pile of beefy men with discernible jockstraps. Cool, huh?

The best part of football is the last part; the interview in the locker room. If you are watching a live telecast, pay close attention. Very close. Like, put down Anne Rice! Often, the camera will accidentally pick up a burly, beefy player holding only a towel in front of him. Sometimes, when the moon is in Aquarius, that towel will accidentally be knocked away from said player.

Proof that there is a God and that He is homosexual.

BASEBALL

Instead of running with a ball in this sport, someone throws a ball at you. Then, if you're lucky, you hit the ball back. If you aren't lucky, the ball hits you. Right on the forehead. Right in public. This is not fun. We know. It happened to us at our brother's Little League game. It hurt like goddamned hell.

Baseball is the ballet of the sports world. It is graceful, even sensual to watch. Yet just when you are most impressed by the balletlike moves, someone spits something large out of their mouth.

But here's the best thing about baseball: All of the players look like *Playgirl* centerfolds! Maybe *Playgirl* should have an all-baseball issue. This sport is so much better than football, where the average weight of a player is thirty tons. We think baseball guys are perfect. Just watch those flying balls!

TENNIS

Tennis is our favorite het sport, or at least the one most of us relate to best. Some of us even play tennis, now and again.

Tennis follows the same basic hetero sports format: A ball is put in motion. Two people sweat a lot and chase the ball around. After a bigillion hours someone wins a really shiny trophy.

Sweat is important in tennis. When a tennis player really sweats, his sexy white shorts and shirt stick right to him. This, at first, may sound gross. But not at all! When the tennis player's white shorts and shirt stick to him, you can see right through his white shorts and shirt. Often, a cameraman will shove his camera right up behind the tennis player. This is called heaven.

Our favorite tennis player of all time is Bjorn Borg. Our second favorite? Stefan Edberg. We love all things Swedish. Did you know Ann-Margret is Swedish?

Our third favorite tennis player is Boris Becker. Boris sweats very well. Boris is a little like a big Irish setter—he falls down all the time. We think that's cute. He can fall on us any time.

SOCCER

Straight American guys have been trying to warm up to this homoerotic European sport for years. Their hearts just aren't in it, really. We'll never see *Monday Night Soccer* on a major network, but we like to surf the sports channels just to catch a glimpse of the uniforms.

GOLF

Little, shriveled white balls and funny pastel pants—this game is a veritable heterosexual showcase. Golf is the least aesthetically pleasing game for the homo audience because of its lack of physical contact among guys. But then there are always fantasies about Tiger Woods or those oversize irons to keep us going.

The only thing scarier and more boring than the game of golf is the clothes golfers wear. Those lime green golf pants and checked golf shirts just have to go—further proof that there should be ordinances against many heterosexual pastimes.

HOCKEY

The word "puck" makes us laugh.

This sport is a burlesque of a misguided heterosexual utopian vision in which everyone lives in Finland and beats the crap out of one another daily. Hockey's testerone level is off the charts.

Not for us. What's the use of watching people on ice if they're not Rudy Galindo? Besides, hockey players do not put their butts into the air nearly as much as football players, and they wear baggy, protective clothing. If only we could see their nipples in the cold, it wouldn't be so bad.

On top of how baggy the hockey uniform is, hockey is the most violent hetero sport after boxing. In fact, most hockey fans are more interested in the bashing of brains and splashing of blood than they are in the score.

Hockey is mega-hetero and violently wholesome. *Mighty Ducks 3*. Need we say more?

TRACK AND FIELD

We like these sports, although we wish they still adhered to the buck-naked dress code established in ancient Greece.

Whether they're flexing their thighs over hurdles, slithering up and over sinuous poles, or passing phallic batons among themselves, we think track-and-field stars are all honorary homos.

BASKETBALL

Shooting hoops is an obsession of many heterosexual men and suburban families. They dribble here, they dribble there, they dribble EVERYWHERE. Basketball players are at least half naked a lot of the time and tend to have flamboyant streaks, causing them to dress in wedding gowns, fuck Madonna, or star in movies with Bugs Bunny. Still, even with these qualifications, we're afraid to say that it is still a hopelessly heterosexual game.

Remember: When the Harlem Globetrotters visited *Gilligan's Island*, they were more interested in Tina Louise than in Bob Denver.

WATER POLO

We at the Institute for Heterosexual Studies have to admit that we aren't sure of either the rules or object of this sport. And our ignorance is not from lack of effort. We slavishly study all water sports. But it seems we keep getting distracted.

Rabidly Heterosexual Sports

There is some crossover in the world of sports—some cross-fertilization, if you will—between the gay and hetero athletic arenas. But certain sporting events hardly ever appeal to nonheterosexuals:

BOXING

This sport shows what straights think of one another. Not much!

Boxing involves hitting someone as hard as you can as often as you can while hopping around like a bunny. Obviously, this is painful for both parties. And yet heterosexuals pay money to cheer on this barbarity.

Gay people do not believe in physical violence. They have perfected verbal violence, which is in its own way much more bloody.

Aside from the ugliness of the sport of boxing there is the aftermath—severe headaches and blood that won't wash out of those flashy trunks no matter how hard you try.

SNOWMOBILING

Cold weather, many layers of clothing, and a chance to scar Mother Earth. Sure, we would love to go snowmobiling—WHEN HELL FREEZES OVER.

HUNTING AND SHOOTING

Heterosexuals like to shoot things. And animals. Shooting qualifies as a sport in the straight world, even though it doesn't depend on sheer strength and agility. The bigger your gun, the more your fun. You'll get a bang out of reading an NRA publication. Try it some time.

BOWLING

Are Fred Flintstone and Ralph Kramden heterosexual dork poster boys or what? The balls are heavy and the shoes are not chic at all. Bowling can sometimes qualify as a camp diversion, but many breeders take it seriously.

FISHING

Even watching Brad Pitt in *A River Runs Through It* can't make us think of this sport as anything but boring, boring, boring. We like fresh fish as much as the next guy, but it's just easier to pop into the nearest sushi place. Now, maybe if they made leather waders . . .

The one interesting thing about this sport is that the main instrument is called a "rod." The rod is a long instrument that is flung out in an attempt to catch and reel in a victim. In this way fishing is much like going to a straight bar on the weekend.

The Straightest Holiday on Earth: Super Bowl Sunday

Super Bowl Sunday is not officially a U.S. holiday. And yet, for all het males and many het females, this day surpasses New Year's Eve and Christmas for excitement. Though often a garish, overproduced event, there is still enough running and tackling to keep heteros happy.

The very first Super Bowl occurred in 1967. The Green Bay Packers defeated the Kansas City Chiefs, 35–10. Previous to the Super Bowl the Big Game was the National Football League championship. The championship game did not give the fans enough of a bang. They need the extra public relations jolt only the Super Bowl could provide.

The best and most hideous thing about the Super Bowl? The halftime entertainment. Through the years a plethora of talented and untalented performers have forged their way through thousands of silly dance numbers and special effects. One former sixties diva was even whisked offstage midperformance by a helicopter. She has not been heard from since.

ASK MR. HETERO!

Dear Mr. Hetero,

Why are straights so into sports?

Dying to Know in Des Moines

Dear Dying,

Watching muscular men in tight clothing tackle one another and then squeal is the closest most heterosexuals get to being homosexual.

Dear Mr. Hetero,

Who are Mike Ditka, Joe Montana, and Joe Namath?

Wondering in Wabash

Dear Wondering,

Mike Ditka invented the ditka paddle, used often in sexual foreplay in the Far East. Joe Montana led the fight against Canada, winning our forty-first state, which Joe somewhat piggishly named after himself. Joe Namath is the brand name of a lip gloss used by transsexual prostitutes in Taiwan.

Dear Mr. Hetero,

Why do heterosexual men so often use sports metaphors and analogies when describing sex?

Without a Clue in Kansas

Dear Without,

The heterosexual male is that unique species that views all things as ultimately about winning or losing and, more sadly, about domination. It is for this reason that the heterosexual mate is often described as "tackled" or "roped." Also, touchdowns and home runs have often more to do with luck than skill, not unlike heterosexual sex. And often an entire inning or quarter can go by without scoring, also not unlike heterosex.

Dear Mr. Hetero,

I've noticed that straight guys often get really nervous around me and my gay pals, especially in the shower room at the gym. What gives?

Passing the Soap in Peoria

Dear Passing,

Want to scare an average hetero male? Just tell him that all the other men in a crowded locker room are from a visiting ballet troupe. The hetero male will automatically back into the nearest corner. If there is no corner, the hetero male will take out brick and mortar and build one.

Why is the hetero male inordinantly protective of his anus? Here are three competing theories:

Theory 1: Straight males believe if something enters their anus they will automatically become pregnant.

Theory 2: Straight males are often embarrassed because their butts aren't as shapely as gay butts.

Theory 3: Straight males secretly know that once penetrated they will become insatiable bottoms and will be beating the streets at all hours looking to sit on anything that moves.

6. They Call It Living: The Straight Lifestyle

WHY DO THEY DRESS SO FUNNY? WHERE DO THEY SHOP AND EAT? CAN YOU TRUST A RESTAURANT WITH HETEROSEXUAL WAITERS?

Here at the Institute, we have devoted a major part of our research to studying the day-to-day life of average heterosexuals. Dreary work, we know, but someone has to do it. And, in the process, we have learned the hard way that we must hire heterosexuals to perform the onerous task of transcribing the data—we lost three trusty gay assistants who were bored to DEATH by the details of this truncated way of life.

In this chapter we have distilled the key elements, hoping to make it possible for you to learn about how heteros live without endangering your health. But if you should begin to feel faint when perusing the details, close the book immediately. Take a deep breath. Go for a walk and buy yourself something nice.

Like any special interest group, straight people have their own, quite insular, set of behavior patterns. Although their way of life might seem aberrant and even shocking to you, remember that they actually enjoy their odd habits and rituals. You have probably seen the Hollywood version of hetero living, especially in *situation comedies*, or *sitcoms*. But in this chapter, we help you identify the essential elements of the hetero lifestyle even when there is no laugh track involved.

It is only shallow people who do not judge by appearances.

—OSCAR WILDE

How Heterosexuals Look

Clothes make the man, but you wouldn't want to make any man dressed like a true hetero.

You can spot a hetero a mile away by his lack of fashion sense. Het men tend to gravitate toward dull, ill-fitting clothes that emphasize their figure flaws or their poor taste. Fortunately, straight guys are largely oblivious to their own fashion impairment, although with the advent of mirrors in the sixteenth century and the proliferation of Armani and Ralph Lauren ads in the nineties, the straight man's inability to take charge of his own appearance continues to baffle experts.

Life is all about choices, and most nonhomosexuals make the wrong ones at the department store. If you are feeling particularly charitable, you might want to take a hetero man shopping. If not, his only hope of rising above the het fashion victim scene is to get married.

Remember, homosexuals invented fashion, so we will always be ahead of the game. We do not recommend staring at poorly dressed heterosexuals—in their culture, clothing is not meant as a feast for the eyes, and you are liable to anger them. However, the following list is useful for het-watching, and for keeping in mind how proud we should be to come from a fashion-savvy culture.

The Shopping Habits of *Homo erectus hetero*

Heterosexuals, by and large, would rather build than shop. Prehistoric heteros killed the first woolly beast that came along, then skinned it and wore its hide for several years. Present-day straight guys show vestiges of this shopping

strategy, although some het males have totally lost the ability to hunt for clothing and instead leave that task to the females of their tribe, specifically spouses, who replenish the men's wardrobes at Christmastime and during holidays celebrating fertility, such as Father's Day.

At least the het's lack of interest in quality shopping keeps the lines at great stores short. But how much overlap is there in our shopping tastes? Not much, as you can see from the following list.

HETERO SHOPPING SPOTS	HOMO SHOPPING SPOTS
Banana Republic	Abercrombie & Fitch
Christian Dior	Christian Lacroix
Polo Sport	Polo
Filene's Basement	Gap outlet
Gap Kids	Gap
Tourneau	Tiffany & Co.
Pier 1 Imports	Pottery Barn
IKEA	IKEA

Extreme Hetero-Wear

They're disgusting. They're outrageous. They seem to have no sense of public decency. Yes, as stereotyped as it may sound, *some* heterosexuals are just flaming kings who have to strut their stuff! Run in the opposite direction whenever one of these passes by:

- Pants with whales or ducks
- Funny little tweed hats
- Black nylon socks
- Pants that show butt cleavage
- Cuban shirts
- Hunting and fishing vests
- Leather sandals with white socks

The Hetero Menu, or What's Cooking at Denny's?

Heterosexuals have strange eating habits. To understand them, think back to how you ate when you were ten years old. You can always be sure to please a het with a bag of Chee•tos and a Yoo-Hoo.

If you want to try doing your own market research on straight eating habits, cruise the aisles of any supermarket. When you come upon a cart, check its contents. Even if a supermarket cart contains no Pampers or tubes of contraceptive gel, you can usually spot a het shopper by other telltale merchandise.

See some milk, white bread, eggs, pudding mix, Jell-O, Velveeta, or Kraft macaroni and cheese? You won't be going home with that guy to listen to Sondheim albums. But spy a tiny basket filled with arugula, a jar of pesto, Rose's Lime Juice, and reduced fat water biscuits, and you might want to hang around at the checkout line behind the guy who's holding it.

ALL-TIME MOST AMAZING STRAIGHT FOOD INVENTIONS

Cheez Whiz
The cheesesteak
Chicken nuggets
Wonderbread
Juice boxes
Fruit Roll-Ups
Tang
Hamburger Helper
Frozen fish sticks
Breakfast burritos
Pringles
Big Mac
Slim Jim
Twinkies
Rice-A-Roni

Straight Restaurants

What can we say about heterosexual dining establishments? Our researchers who must make field trips to these faux food emporiums receive combat pay. While there are some rumors that all straight restaurants in the country get their menus items shipped in from the same frozen food warehouse in Secaucus, we know that this is not true. The warehouse is in Scranton.

Next year our food researchers will be teaming up with the Zagat's people to produce a guide, *Gay Men Don't Eat Fajitas*, which will help all of us steer away from those ultrastraight dining experiences that leave you bloated and zoned out on Muzak. In our preface to that volume, we offer the

TEN WARNING SIGNS THAT YOU ARE IN A STRAIGHT RESTAURANT

1. The restaurant is right next to a highway exit.
2. It has a ridiculously cute pseudo-ethnic name, usually Irish.
3. They have a kiddie placemat/menu.
4. Some of the sandwiches are named after sitcom characters.
5. The restaurant is in Walt Disney World.
6. The waitrons wear funny hats.
7. There is a brochure available explaining the heart-warming story of the owner's American dream.
8. It advertises on television.
9. The menu boasts forty-seven varieties of chicken wings.
10. The guys at the bar weigh four hundred pounds.

STRAIGHT DINNER SPOTS

Red Lobster
Friendly's
T.G.I. Friday's
The Chart House
Houlihan's
Applebee's
Hamburger Hamlet

ETHNIC FOOD FOR STRAIGHTS

Chi-Chi's

Chili's

Taco Bell

Olive Tree

Bagel Boss

DELIGHTFUL STRAIGHT BRUNCH SPOTS

Bob Evans

Denny's

Bob's Big Boy

Bennigan's

ASK MR. HETERO!

Dear Mr. Hetero,
What is a "Happy Meal"?

Pink Highway Traveler

Dear Pink,

Well, to me, it is a grilled portobello mushroom on focaccia. But I believe you're referring to an odd heterosexual enticement practiced by fast-food establishments. Children receive small fried things in a bag containing a very special toy that will soon find its way to the landfills of America. I know it is hard to imagine, but try. A homosexual equivalent would be a small jar of beluga in a leather pouch also containing a flavored condom.

Mr. Hetero,

Can you get sick eating food prepared by heterosexuals?

Keen to Know in Key West

Dear Keen,

No, if you make wise choices. Heterosexuals are masters of red meat, but I wouldn't let them prepare anything else. Ordering tuna carpaccio from a straight chef is asking for trouble.

Dear Mr. Hetero,

What should I feed a heterosexual if he drops in unexpectedly?

Bare Cupboard in Barrington

Dear Bare,

Well, remember—we advised against feeding these exotic creatures in the first chapter. But if you know some straight people and they come inside your house, say, to watch something on television, you can't go wrong offering them high-fat, high-sodium snack food. Straights are infamous for their consumption of fattening munchies. That's why they are often overweight, and their fingers taste salty.

Mealtime

Not only do homosexuals and heterosexuals eat different foods and consume different beverages, they also take a different amount of time doing it. We at the Institute for Heterosexual Studies share our scientific evidence:

Breakfast

HOMO: Three minutes (protein shake)

HETERO: Thirty minutes (Bacon, eggs, toast, coffee)

Lunch

HOMO: Three minutes (protein shake)

HETERO: Thirty minutes (No. 3 Combo; McDonald's)

Dinner

HOMO: Three hours (grilled tuna over angel hair pasta with Bill and Glenn and Bruce and Ted)

HETERO: Twenty minutes (Hamburger Helper with Min, Heather, and Biff)

HETEROSEXUAL SPICES

- Ketchup
- A.1. steak sauce
- Tabasco
- Salt

AROUND THE HOUSE: HETERO VS. HOMO APPLIANCES

HETERO: Mr. Coffee coffeemaker
HOMO: Braun coffeemaker

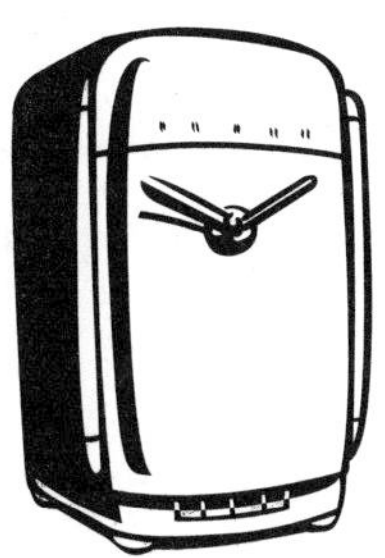

HETERO: Microwave
HOMO: Cuisinart

HETERO: Eureka vacuum
HOMO: Miele vacuum

HETERO VS. HOMO DINING

First Course
HETERO: Pigs in a blanket
HOMO: Red caviar

Second Course
HETERO: Chee•tos
HOMO: Orange fennel salad

Third Course
HETERO: Chicken pot pie (frozen)
HOMO: Roast duck quarters with cracked black pepper

Fourth Course
HETERO: Dole pineapple slices
HOMO: Layered raspberries and ladyfingers

Beverage
HETERO: Schlitz
HOMO: Louis Jadot

ASK MR. HETERO!

Dear Mr. Hetero,

I've heard that behind our backs straights are secretive. Can you tell me some straight secrets?

Questioning in Queens

Dear Questioning,

Most straight "secrets" are of a sexual nature. Because of this, I think it best not to let the cat out of the bag. (So to speak.) Straights keep secrets because they are shame-based. And really, can you blame them?

Dear Mr. Hetero,

My neighbor, whom I'll call Stan, is overflowing with hetero self-loathing. He's a real downer. He follows my lover Bill and me around the gym. He begs us to join him at the mall. He is envious of every facet of our admittedly fabulous lifestyle.

Recently, out of pity, we invited Stan to our Academy Awards party. What a mistake! Stan ruined the evening by getting drunk and trying to keep up with the gay dish. Let's face it, a drunken straight man has no business criticizing Jodie Foster's fashion sense. Stan was clearly out of his element.

Now that we've had Stan to one event, he expects to come to every tiny dinner party we throw. Who knew straights were such leeches? Our question is, can we let Stan down easy or do we have to put the house on the market?

Saddened in Saginaw

Dear Saddened,

As you yourself have discovered, give a het an inch, he takes a mile. Obviously, in their natural element, straights can be somewhat amusing and even helpful. (Heteros were great during my last flat tire.) But a line has to be drawn somewhere. In my home I don't even let some homosexuals venture opinions, especially during something as important as the Oscars. I say, get Stan to put his house on the market and don't answer the phone.

P.S. I thought Jodie looked super—stately and sexy.

Heterosexuals often get together in public places. This is good for them. It makes them feel less lonely. Being straight can be a very lonely road to travel. Our many linguistic research fellows have listened in as straight people practice their witty repartee in bars.

PICKUP LINES IN STRAIGHT BARS

"I'll pay for the sitter."

"You sure have taken the weight off from your pregnancy."

"You're so funny. You should be a radio talk-show host."

"The red Corvette Stingray is mine."

"Bartender, her next five Jagermeisters are on me."

"Wanna see a trick I learned in the navy?"

"It gets a lot bigger when you touch it."

"I was in the top fiftieth percentile of my two-year college."

"I went to Dartmouth for one semester. The chicks were ugly."

"I love children. The more, the merrier."

7. Heterosexual Amusements

Do heterosexuals really have fun? Or, "Honey, where is the remote?"

Playing Straight: Their Leisure Pursuits

Straight folks can't spend all their time tackling one another, replicating themselves, or hitting balls around. They must find other diversions. In this respect, they are much like us—they listen to music, go to the movies, and some are even known to read a book now and then. You can learn a lot about their culture by exploring their amusements. Maybe even more than you want to know.

Music

Straights gravitate toward two distinctive types of music: *insipid* or *unbearable.*

Insipid: Masters of this soft rock genre include Christopher Cross, Paul Anka, Paul Williams, Jim Croce, or any of the various Eagles.

ALL-TIME INSIPID HETERO HITS

"Arthur's Theme"

"Born Free"

"Cat's in the Cradle"
"Danke Schoen"
"Endless Love"
"Evergreen"
"It Was a Very Good Year"
"Moon River"
"My Way"
"Sailing"
"Strangers in the Night"
"Time in a Bottle"

Unbearable: Heavy metal, a *totally straight invention*. The only good thing to be said about heavy metal is that the guitars are often loud enough to drown out the insipid lyrics. Though drowning out the lyrics in straight music is not a bad idea, it's not as good as drowning out the lyrics *and* the music. Which we call silence. Silence is always preferable to heavy metal hetero music. Better than silence is Sondheim. But that's another story and another book.

Grunge music is heavy metal recorded less well. Grunge is mostly homo friendly. The late Kurt Cobain often wished he was homosexual. (Courtney Love will do that to you.)

HETERO MUSIC	HOMO MUSIC
AC/DC	ABBA
Billy Joel	Elton John
Petula Clark	Dusty Springfield
Celine Dion	Barbra Streisand
Loretta Lynn	Patsy Cline
Smashing Pumpkins	Smashing Pumpkins
Eddie Vedder	Morrissey
Bush	REM
Carly Simon	Joni Mitchell

MUSIC NO ONE WILL CLAIM

Michael Jackson

La Toya Jackson

Wayne Newton

HETERO SONGS WITH HOMO OVERTONES

"A Boy Named Sue"

"Baubles, Bangles and Beads"

"Beat It"

"Come On-a My House"

"Doctor Feelgood"

"Dude Looks Like a Lady"

"He's Got the Whole World in His Hands"

"Son of a Preacher Man"

"To Sir with Love"
"Layla"
"Touch Me in the Morning"
"Where the Boys Are"

ASK MR. HETERO!

Dear Mr. Hetero,

Aside from k.d. lang, does gay country music exist?

Opie from Opryland

Dear Opie,

Country music songs usually dwell on such deep topics as cheating wives, fast cars, and excessive consumption of beer. For this reason, country is, along with rap and heavy metal, a totally heterosexual construct. We'd like to see a country song with the word "construct" in it. Guess we'll have to call Lyle Lovett.

Dear Mr. Hetero,

The other day I was watching a Jackie O documentary and I began to sob. She was such a class act. There is no one like her today. My lover Felix, who was hetero for years in the army, began to tease and make fun of me. Felix says Jackie was nothing but a Barbie doll and never contributed anything lasting to culture. This sent me over the edge. I've been locked in the bedroom for two days. (Luckily, there happened to be Girl Scout cookies under the bed.) Felix is vowing to call the police if I don't open the door. He apologizes relentlessly and has offered to do anything I ask to repair our relationship, even that position in bed he thought might hurt his neck. But, geeze, I don't know. It wasn't as if he dissed Jackie jokingly. He really meant it. He thinks she was "just an icon." I rejoined, "I suppose you think Marilyn was JUST an icon! Or Jimmy Dean!" Felix was about to answer yes, when I closed the bedroom door and locked it. My point is, if he can't understand how grace and beauty add to the world, how can he understand anything—and how can he really be gay? I think he's just pretending to be gay. All of his siblings and his father and everyone in his army troop were gay. Couldn't he just be trying to fit in?

Hurt in Hawaii

Dear Hurt,

We went through the same thing with our ex, Jason. For neither love nor money could we get Jason to understand the real importance of Dusty Springfield. We did everything we could to bring him around: We drew diagrams on the chalkboard, took him on field trips to record stores, showed him arcles in the *New York Times Magazine*. Finally, we played *Dusty in Memphis* nonstop for seven nights and seven days. It was all for naught. Jason was just immune to la Springfield. We were torn apart. In all other ways Jason was an angel. He was great and giving in bed. He liked everything else we liked. He even got the social significance of other sixties divas—Ronnie and Lulu and Petula. He just did not get THE sixties diva, Dusty. We thought long and hard. We prayed. We went on retreat. We saw our therapist twice a week. We even called our mother. But finally, we had to face facts and give Jason the heave-ho.

Jason took it very badly. He even pretended to have come round to la Springfield. He would stand outside our apartment window and sing "Wishin' and Hopin' " until the police inevitably came. But we knew Jason was not converted. A true Dusty-ite would never in one million years actually *sing* one of *her* songs. Or, sing along to one of her songs. Or, the absolute worst, *whistle* to one of her songs.

We admit we miss Jason. We miss his smile. His eagerness. His butt. But, whenever we are most overcome with Jason-longing, we simply put "I Just Don't Know What to Do with Myself" on the stereo. Before long we are dancing around the room muttering to ourselves, "Jason who?"

Straight Lit: What Do They Read?

Even though we all know that homosexuals make the best writers, straight authors continue to pop onto the best-seller list. In fact, many best-sellers tend to celebrate the heterosexual lifestyle ad nauseam. You should check them out: They contain a treasure trove of information about how heterosexuals make it through the long and weary day.

ALL-TIME STRAIGHT BEST-SELLERS

The Bridges of Madison Country
The Rules
Iron John
The Christmas Box
Men Are from Mars, Women Are from Venus
The Stand
The Bible
From Here to Eternity
For Whom the Bell Tolls

In the world of authors, the difference between heterosexuality and homosexuality is quite pronounced. For example, Norman Mailer is the most hetero writer of all time.

Some say this is because he writes with his penis, which is very small. Others say it is because Gore Vidal scares him.

Norman Mailer follows in a long heterosexual tradition that reached its nadir with Ernest "Papa" Hemingway. Papa may have been a latent homosexual who wrote overcompensating macho works of fiction. His mommy dressed him up in girl's clothes when he was little. Later in life Hemingway was driven to shooting defenseless animals, eventually including himself. He also created characters who all seemed male, even when they were supposed to be female nurses. What do you think all of this means? We have no idea, but offer the following for your consideration.

HETERO WRITERS	HOMO WRITERS
Norman Mailer	Gore Vidal
John Updike	John Cheever
Arthur Miller	Edward Albee
Eugene O'Neill	Tennessee Williams
David Mamet	Terrence McNally
Saul Bellow	Truman Capote
August Wilson	Lanford Wilson

The straight community loves to read magazins. They buy many of their magazines at the checkout counter of the local supermarket, a heterosexual oasis. Lurid publications such as the *Globe*, the *Star*, and the *National Enquirer* are full of lies and make famous people look like idiotic children.

Magazines, along with television, are a perfect way for the straight world to hold a mirror up to itself. Surprisingly, this is not frightening or heartbreaking to them. We don't get it. But that is why our work at the Institute for Heterosexual Studies is never finished.

STRAIGHT MAGAZINES

Bowling Digest
Bride's
Chic
Cycle World
Golf Illustrated
Hustler
Inside Golf
Maternity Fashions
Metropolitan Life
Penthouse
Playboy
Soap Opera Weekly

Sports Illustrated
Super Bike
Wrestling Illustrated

Movies for Breeders

Heterosexual teenagers go to the movies in droves. Indeed, we have these hormone-driven straight teens to thank for the careers of Bruce Willis, Arnold Schwarzenegger, Sylvester Stallone, Jim Carey, Steven Seagal, Adam Sandler, Tom Arnold, and countless others we have blocked from our memory.

Some older heterosexuals also go to the movies sometimes, when they can get a baby-sitter. But, like their teenage counterparts, they prefer different types of films than we do. At the Institute, we will often screen a straight movie and a gay movie back to back, just to help us keep our perspective on why homosexuals should rule the world.

HETERO MOVIES	HOMO MOVIES
The Bodyguard	*Diva*
Ghost	*Truly, Madly, Deeply*
The Big Chill	*Longtime Companion*

Ordinary People	*Home for the Holidays*
The Shawshank Redemption	*Midnight Express*
The Black Stallion	*Equus*
Terms of Endearment	*The Turning Point*
A Passage to India	*A Room with a View*
Howards End	*Maurice*
Doctor Zhivago	*Lawrence of Arabia*
Rocky	*The Rocky Horror Picture Show*
The Sound of Music	*Cabaret*
Drugstore Cowboy	*Midnight Cowboy*
Bonnie and Clyde	*The Living End*
Summer and Smoke	*Suddenly, Last Summer*
Uncle Buck	*Auntie Mame*
Woodstock	*Wigstock*

HETERO MOVIE STARS	**HOMO MOVIE STARS**
Doris Day	Rock Hudson
Tony Curtis	Tony Randall
Bruce Willis	Jean-Claude Van Damme

Sharon Stone
Jodie Foster
William H. Macy
Austin Pendleton
Kevin Bacon
Kevin Spacey
Beethoven
Benji
Sir Laurence Olivier
Sir John Gielgud
Charles Bronson
Charles Laughton
Marlon Brando
Montgomery Clift
Loretta Young
Barbara Stanwyck
Chris O'Donnell
Rosie O'Donnell
King Kong
Godzilla

RELENTLESSLY HETERO CHARACTERS

Captain Ahab
James Bond
Braveheart
Rhett Butler
Rambo
La Femme Nikita
The Terminator

Some movie stars scream their straightness. This can be deafening. We encourage them to whisper in the future. When stars scream their sexual preference too much, we automatically become suspect. We don't mean to. It's just the way we are. We at the Institute for Heterosexual Studies think the following stars doth protest too much.

BEYOND HETERO

Angela Bassett
Warren Beatty
Sean Connery
Kirk Douglas
Michael Douglas
Mel Gibson
Roger Moore
Sean Penn
Kurt Russell
Will Smith
Sylvester Stallone

Often the combination of two straight stars makes them so sexually alluring, one forgets their sexual persuasion. We like it when this happens. We wish it happened more often. The following couples are also invited for merlot under the moonlight. Even Larry and Viv. Heck, we're not afraid of ghosts. We liked Patrick Swayze as one a lot.

HETEROEROTIC

Susan Sarandon and Tim Robbins
Agents Scully and Muldaur
David Bowie and Iman
Laurence Olivier and Vivien Leigh
Jessica Lange and Sam Shepard

Johnny Depp and Kate Moss
Paul Newman and Robert Redford
Matt LeBlanc and Matthew Perry

The Black Box of Life: TV

Television was invented so that heterosexuals wouldn't have to go out after dark.

Because television can be enjoyed at home, in the privacy of one's La-Z-Boy, it takes the place of most other art forms in heterosexual culture. Have you ever heard a heterosexual mention the name Puccini? He probably thinks it is a pasta noodle. Straights are horrendously operaphobic. Ditto the theater. Ditto art. But television is right up their alley.

Most of pre-*Ellen* television reflected the hetero lifestyle. Television, for straights, is a narcotic that keeps them from becoming too aggressive.

Late-night TV is a veritable hetero wasteland where testosterone rules. It's as if all the hetero boys who beat the shit out of you back in grade school grew up and decided to become talk-show hosts. The choices are an angry Dave Letterman, an infantile Leno, a smug Billy Maher, an earnest Ted, a mischievous Conan, or that TV personality that won't die: Tom Snyder.

Of these choices, our favorite source of heterosexual comedy at the Institute is Dave. We keep trying to get him to come speak here, to lead seminars on the hetero lifestyle. Dave is so straight, you sometimes think he might explode. Dave is straight and he wants to make sure we don't forget it.

We don't.

TOP TEN REASONS LETTERMAN IS OBVIOUSLY STRAIGHT

10. He drools over Drew Barrymore's breasts and championship sports figures.
9. Those cigars.
8. Madonna scares him.
7. Harvey Fierstein scares him.
6. Charlie Sheen doesn't scare him.
5. He hasn't renamed his dogs Uma and Oprah yet.
4. His target audience is fifteen-year-old boys.
3. He stomps around when something stupid doesn't get a laugh.
2. He looks uncomfortable in tasteful suits.
1. He fears and loathes Richard Simmons.

Like movies and books, some TV shows are relentlessly straight. These shows usually involve: (a) guns, (b) cars, (c) blond bimbos, and (d) trench coats.

THE HETEROSEXUAL TELEVISION HALL OF FAME

Bonanza
Three's Company
Full House
Baywatch
Championship Wrestling
Married with Children
America's Funniest Home Videos
Charlie's Angels
Dr. Quinn, Medicine Woman
Dragnet
Home Improvement
Mad TV
Monday Night Football
Rawhide
World's Strongest Man Competition

TELEVISION WE AGREE ON

The Brady Bunch
Frasier

Friends

Mad About You

The Mary Tyler Moore Show

Party of Five

Relativity

Seinfeld

3rd Rock from the Sun

The X-Files

GAY TV

Some TV has a homo sensibility:

Absolutely Fabulous

Bewitched

Anything on AMC

Cybill

Ellen

Melrose Place

Pee-wee's Playhouse

Roseanne

The Rosie O'Donnell Show

The Simpsons

The Wild, Wild West

World Figure Skating Championships

Travel: The Hetero Circuit

Believe it or not, there is actually a straight travel circuit. There are even straight circuit queen families. In the winter or spring, they go to Walt Disney World. Summer finds them at a lakeside or beach cabin or at one of our national parks. Come fall, they take in the foliage. Of course, some travel is not seasonal, which explains The Mall of America.

Actually, for just about every great homosexual travel spot, there is a heterosexual equivalent. We list them so you won't make the mistake of going to one of them.

HETERO TRAVEL	HOMO TRAVEL
Atlantic City	Provincetown
Niagara Falls	Montreal
Vietnam War Memorial	The AIDS Quilt
Graceland	Liberace Museum
Alaska Cruises	Rainbow Cruises

Branson, Missouri
Orlando
Milford Plaza
Curaçao
Fort Lauderdale
Mardi Gras, New Orleans
Grand Canyon
Tijuana
San Diego
Giza, Egypt
Corfu

Hotlanta
Key West
Algonquin
Cancún
South Beach

Mardi Gras, Sydney
Russian River
San Miguel de Allende
San Francisco
Ibiza, Spain
Mykonos

Playing Straight: A Cautionary Tale

At the Institute for Heterosexual Studies, our Department of Current Affairs is tracking many issues throughout the country. One of these is the shocking story of the straight Hollywood closet—gay actors forced to play straight roles to earn megabucks at the box office.

One of our interviewers on the West Coast turned in this strange interview with a handsome young fellow we will call "Actor X." As you will see, the Institute staffer caught this young thespian at a turning point, when he was having trouble living with the lie that had made him famous and wealthy.

INTERVIEWER

Let me start by saying how convincing you were as a macho heterosexual in your last movie.

ACTOR X

Thanks.

INTERVIEWER

By my count, you blew up three buildings, torched ten police cars and jumped off a forty-story building with your Native American partner.

ACTOR X

Actually, my double—Phillipe—did most of that. But I did scratch my elbow going through a revolving door.

INTERVIEWER

Ouch!

ACTOR X

Exactly.

INTERVIEWER

So, in other words, you don't have to be one to play one.

ACTOR X

No. Acting is acting.

INTERVIEWER

Are you afraid you'll be typecast?

ACTOR X

I would hope the industry is beyond that.

INTERVIEWER

What do you think of when you have to kiss a straight?

ACTOR X

My country.

INTERVIEWER

Did you have to dumb down to play one?

ACTOR X

No. I've been lucky in that I've met lots of straights who are surprisingly bright.

Interviewer falls out of his chair.

INTERVIEWER

I'm sorry. Did you say . . . *lots*?

ACTOR X

Many.

INTERVIEWER

Many?

ACTOR X

Some.

INTERVIEWER

We'll have to get you a job at the Institute.

ACTOR X

What I'm trying to say is that they're really people like you and me. Only—

INTERVIEWER

Dumber.

ACTOR X

That isn't the word I would use.

INTERVIEWER

Slower.

ACTOR X

That's not the word either.

INTERVIEWER

Less evolved.

ACTOR X

Okay. Yes. That works.

INTERVIEWER

Did you find yourself carrying your role home with you?

ACTOR X

I did. I thought Max would kill me.

INTERVIEWER

Max is your lover.

ACTOR X

Poodle.

INTERVIEWER

In closing, do you have any similar advice for other actors playing similar roles?

ACTOR X

Yes. Be careful of your waist. Those six packs of beer every night add up and it's not pretty.

INTERVIEWER

Thank you. This has been very enlightening.

ACTOR X

Really? I barely thought I scratched the surface.

INTERVIEWER

Speaking of scratching surfaces, what's up after the interview?

Interviewer leers at Actor X. Actor X becomes uncomfortable.

ACTOR X

I . . . Let's see. I have. Oh. Right. Shiatsu. Then, lunch with my agent. *Sorry*.

INTERVIEWER

I could give you a lift.

ACTOR X

(Nervously) I have my Jag.

Interviewer looks out the window.

INTERVIEWER

Yes, I can see your Jag from here. Wait. Isn't that your costar in the front seat? What's her name?

ACTOR X

(*Nervously*) Laura is a friend. Strictly. We're friends.

Pause.

INTERVIEWER

I smell a fish.

ACTOR X

Okay. All right. If I admit something, will you promise not to tell anyone?

INTERVIEWER

The Institute is a scientific organization. A think tank. We don't gossip.

ACTOR X

This would kill my career if it got out.

INTERVIEWER

Like I said, we aren't gossips.

ACTOR X

I'm straight.

Interviewer falls out of his seat.

ACTOR X

It's been gnawing at me. I had to tell someone.

Interviewer is speechless.

ACTOR X

You don't understand. None of the Lavender Mafia would hire me to play a straight if they knew I was straight.

INTERVIEWER

But you were just at the GLAAD dinner with that actor from *Party of Five*. You're telling me your whole career is a lie?

ACTOR X

I think *lie* is a pretty strong word.

INTERVIEWER

I don't.

ACTOR X

Listen. When the industry thought I was straight I couldn't get an audition to save my life. Not to mention a dinner invitation. Do you have any idea how difficult it is for a *straight actor* to get invited to anything fun in Hollywood? Oh, sure, if you're Kurt and Goldie. Otherwise, forget it. They think straight people can't hold up their end of the conversation.

INTERVIEWER

But you're so convincing as a gay playing straight. Don't you think the public is enlightened enough to accept you as a straight playing straight?

ACTOR X

No.

A car honks.

ACTOR X

Listen. I'm sorry. Laura's got an audition. Thanks for keeping this under our hat.

INTERVIEWER

We never gossip.

Actor X shakes interviewer's hand.

ACTOR X

Let me know if you need help getting a table at Morton's.

Actor X exits. Interviewer picks up the phone and dials.

INTERVIEWER

Hello. This is Sean at the Institute for Heterosexual Studies. Liz Smith, please. Hello, Liz? Have I got some dish for you!

OTHER USEFUL VOLUMES FROM THE INSTITUTE FOR HETEROSEXUAL STUDIES

If you loved this book, you'll want to order

The Gay Guide to Minivans
Will you be forced to ride in one of these things sometime soon? Here's a complete look at how these ugly behemoths allow hetero families to take the playroom and basement on the road with them. Includes advice on finding your way out of one if you ever get lost inside.

The Gay Guide to Malls
Answers the following questions: Are shopping malls merely halfway houses for juvenile delinquents? How many cinnamon buns can heterosexuals really eat? How liberal, really, is the Piercing Pagoda?

The Gay Guide to the Family Room

Do you ever get a yen to build yourself a really campy hetero den in which you and your friends can lounge about, ironically watching Nick at Nite? Well, now you can. It's all here—tips on choosing the BarcaLounger and the fifty-inch TV, finding the right hideous plaid fabrics, and making the important decisions about drop ceilings, paneling, and wet bars.

The Gay Guide to Disney World

"Joe Blow, you've just won a gold medal for being the most heterosexual man on this planet. What are you gonna do now?" "I'M GOING TO DISNEY WORLD!" Handy tips on how to navigate your way through this heterosexual paradise without going nuts.

About the Authors

C.E. Crimmins has written more than a dozen humor books, including *When My Parents Were My Age, They Were Old* and *Madonna and Child: A Maternally Hip Baby Book.* Crimmins is the coauthor, with Tom Maeder, of *Newt Gingrich's Bedtime Stories, The Private Diary of Scarlett O'Hara, The Seven Habits of Highly Defective People,* and *Beyond Star Trek: The Final Degeneration.* Crimmins lives in Philadelphia, the City of Brotherly Love.

Tom O'Leary is an award-winning playwright whose works have been produced in New York, Los Angeles, and Philadelphia. His plays have been published in the magazine *Arts and Understanding*. His two latest comedies, *The Negative Room* and *The Guest House Diaries*, enjoyed very successful runs in Provincetown, Massachussetts, where he lived until recently relocating to Los Angeles.